WHAT
EVERY
LEADER
NEEDS

The Ten Universal and
Indisputable Competencies of
Leadership Effectiveness

Adam C. Bandelli, Ph.D.

ISBN 978-1-63630-136-5 (Paperback)
ISBN 978-1-63630-137-2 (Hardcover)
ISBN 978-1-63630-138-9 (Digital)

Covenant Books, Inc.
11661 Hwy 707
Murrells Inlet, SC 29576
www.covenantbooks.com

What People Are Saying

We don't always expect a look inside the sphere of corporate management to evoke such humane behaviors, but Adam Bandelli's *What Every Leader Needs* harvests ten teachable attributes of leadership that provide a framework for his case studies from the workplace. Steeped in self-awareness-based leadership development, drawing on real-world examples from Bandelli's two decades of coaching, the narrative is as empathetic as it is instructive. It's a workbook to highlight and return to for any dedicated student of leadership.

—Dr. Randall P. White
Chair of Leadership at eMBA HEC Paris and Doha
and coauthor of *Breaking the Glass Ceiling*

What Every Leader Needs is a user's manual that provides an advanced course in leadership. It provides a wealth of specific advice that is evidence based from a leadership expert who has worked with leaders at all levels. Not only does the book provide a list of the ten main competencies that successful leaders have, but it also provides a step-by-step roadmap for how to develop each one.

—Dr. Paul Spector
Professor Emeritus at Muma College of
Business, University of South Florida

I have known Adam for years, and I can confidently say that *What Every Leader Needs* is a master course on leadership from a man who lives out the ideals in this book. It's difficult to find fresh insights on the topic of leadership, but Adam delivers them in every chapter. If you are looking to grow as a leader, look no further!

—Pastor Dave Murphy
Founding and lead pastor of Vital Church and author of
*Undefeated: Conquering Your Doubts and
Living in God's Fullness*

Dr. Bandelli's fluid writing style makes the reader feel that they have personal access to a well-regarded leadership coach. He effectively synthesizes elements of theory, research, and practice to ground leadership concepts. The utilization of 'action-steps' enables the reader to personalize the competencies and serves as a blueprint for one's own leadership development.

—Dr. Robert M. Chell
Professor Emeritus of Psychology at
Fairleigh Dickinson University

Adam Bandelli has masterfully distilled dozens and dozens of books and articles on leadership competencies into an easy-to-read, insightful, and engaging book. This is the kind of book that people can adopt and take personal action on. This book will not become dusty on my bookshelf!

—Dr. Linda Amper
President and CEO of LA Consulting

I can say from my twenty-five years of teaching experience at different universities and as an Imam and leader in the Muslim community in Washington metropolitan area that the message in *What Every Leader Needs* can change and improve your leadership. Moreover, the ten valuable leadership skills discussed can make a huge difference in managing your team and leading your organization. It is a must-read for every leader.

—Dr. Mohamed E. Hassan
President and CEO of Prince William Islamic Center

Dr. Bandelli has masterfully captured a lifetime of leadership principles and practices in a format that both captivates and educates. As an executive coach and management consultant, he has the knowledge and ability to share real-world examples of how diverse leaders think and grow that will help any individual become the best version of themselves. This book is a must-have for your professional library!

—Phillip Chacra
Senior Vice President of Best Buy

Adam's gift is storytelling. Each leader example paints a picture for the reader and gives a real-life story on how the competencies are lived, experienced, or learned. He supports the learning of anyone who picks up this book by describing models, research, programs, and a step-by-step approach on how to develop as a leader. His years of experience, his wealth of knowledge, and his appreciation of leaders he has met along the way let us get to know the author as well as his clients. To be able to have so many examples of leadership in action makes it a pleasure to read.

—Lyne Desormeaux
Consulting psychologist, master coach, and CEO
of Desormeaux Leadership Consulting LLC

In the world of sports, leadership is so critical to the success of any organization. Dr. Bandelli's perspective on leadership is both informative and inspiring to any professional sports team. He takes leadership concepts and makes them easy to apply in a variety of settings. This book is something our team will come back to again and again.

—Stephen Venditti
Director of video at New York Giants

Adam captures the essence of leadership in his book *What Every Leader Needs: The Ten Universal and Indisputable Competencies of Leadership Effectiveness*. It is an easy read with a wealth of information and perspective from his real-life experiences both personally and professionally. The best thing about the book is that it outlines leadership effectiveness that will not only help you excel in business but provide a roadmap for success in all aspects of your life. There's a saying in golf: the most important shot is the next one! Focus on that next shot, read Adam's book, and set yourself up for your best round in business and in life.

—Ed Walls
PGA, Renaissance Country Club, Head Golf Professional

Dr. Bandelli has done a lot of work for those who are continuously growing as leaders. Instead of reading through pages of research to find the few competencies that matter most, he has given you the list based on sound data and illustrated through his experience as a management consultant. Take the time and effort to see how each of the competencies enhances your own personal style and how you can use them to be an even more effective leader.

—Dr. Greg Pennington
Managing partner at Pennpoint Consulting Group

Adam Bandelli not only provides a classic, crystal-clear blueprint for aspiring leaders, but he also coaches us chapter by chapter to take command of ourselves. Practical and timely, Dr. Bandelli has written a book that is sorely needed for our leaderless times.

—Dr. Justin DeSenso
Assistant professor of English and African
American Studies at Penn State Berks

To Kat.
This book would not have been possible without all
your love, encouragement, and support. You inspire me
to be a better leader of our family and our firm. More
importantly, you inspire me to be a better man.

CONTENTS

ACKNOWLEDGMENTS

Every leader whom I have worked with has had a positive impact on my world. To those who helped shape me in college, thank you for seeing my talent and helping to cultivate it. To those early in my career, thank you for helping to lay the foundation for the work that I do. It was an honor to be mentored by each of you. And to all those I work with today, thank you for inspiring me to stay sharp and always on my game.

INTRODUCTION

*If your actions inspire others to dream more, learn more,
do more, and become more, you are a leader.*
—John Quincy Adams

Leadership matters. Without it, people fail. As a leadership and management consultant for over twenty years, I've come across many different leaders with a vast array of unique leadership styles. Some leaders have a certain way about them. They are passionate about their mission and have a vision for the future. They galvanize those around them through inspiration and a burning desire to win. These leaders understand how to build relationships; they look to connect with people at an individual level. They also possess strong self-awareness and know what their strengths and areas of opportunity are. These leaders persevere through good and bad times. They know how to handle challenges and adversity. They learn from experience and strive to get better each day. Some leaders struggle with the impact they desire to have on others. We've all seen those who lead with an iron fist—those who push for results through fear and intimidation. I've never seen these types of leaders succeed in the long-term. They may get the short-term result, but it has a huge negative impact on their ability to lead people over time.

As I've come across leaders from Fortune 50 companies all the way down to small nonprofits, I have started to see certain leadership competencies emerge. These behaviors span across industry and level of leadership. It does not matter if you're a line manager or a CEO; the behaviors apply to all those interested in leading others. These are learned behaviors. They are competencies any leader can learn and put into practice with focus and repetition. In this book, I would like

13

to share my experiences of these leadership competencies with you. I would like to take you through the ten competencies that are indispensable for successful leadership. If you want to have a sustainable positive impact on people, you will put these behaviors into practice.

Before we get into the competencies, it is important to highlight how these skills were selected as the ten universal and indisputable leadership competencies. The information outlined in this book spans over two decades of research on leadership behaviors, skills, and competencies. Our research team conducted a content analysis of hundreds of leadership competency models across different industries, sectors, and organizational levels. From C-suite executives down to first-time managers, the ten dimensions outlined in this book were the common themes across all of the data analysis. Obviously, the content analysis did not include every single leadership model that is out there. We tried to get as many as we could from various management consulting firms, the academic sector, and mainstream literature on leadership. As our research showed us, these ten competency dimensions showed up in some shape or form across most of the models we reviewed. These universal dimensions also apply to leaders across geographical and international regions. Our data analysis led us to the conclusion that these competencies are indisputable. Every leader regardless of industry, geography, or organizational level needs to possess these skills on some level in order to drive success.

We begin with vision. Vision enables leaders to have a clear picture of the future. It helps to pull people together and focus on collective outcomes. It propels a team's mission and purpose. It gives people something to rally behind. Vision includes building a playbook (i.e., putting a plan together for how you intend to make your vision become a reality). It involves bringing others along. No one can accomplish a vision on their own. We need others to get there. We need others for support, encouragement, and counsel. Lastly, vision is about celebrating the successes along the way. It is about setting and achieving small goals that lead us down the right path and then sharing the victories with those who matter most.

From vision, we move to passion. Galileo once said that "passion is the genesis of genius." It is the thing that drives us to accomplish our deepest desires and interests. Passion is about following our pleasures and gratifications—the things that get us energized and excited. It is about leveraging our strengths and maximizing our potential. It is about connecting what drives us to our purpose and mission. Leadership without passion is simply management. Passion brings enthusiasm and a burning desire for anticipating the possibilities of the future.

Commitment is about remaining focused on our goals and objectives. It is about never giving up. We may need to make changes and adjustments along the way, but every leader must model commitment in how they handle issues that surface, in how they handle adversity and difficult experiences. Commitment is also about not using excuses. It is a results-oriented leadership competency and compels leaders to constantly move things forward.

From commitment, we move to vigilance. This is all about execution and being disciplined in our efforts. Leaders need to have specific objectives that they are looking to accomplish—objectives that are specific and measurable, those that they can attain and build upon. The vigilant focus has to be realistic and time-bound. Vigilance is also about accountability. It is about holding ourselves to a high standard and finding people who will push us to achieve our goals when obstacles surface. Lastly, vigilance is about prioritization. It is about putting first things first. We cannot set a vision and do it all. Priorities and delegation are key.

Consistency is about principles, ethics, and integrity. It is about walking one's talk and not changing one's leadership style to meet short-term demands. It is about treating people with respect and dignity and making sure others experience the same approach to leadership day in and day out. Leaders who do not demonstrate consistency in how they think, act, and behave run into problems with their people. They fail to lead with integrity.

Endurance is about following the path that one has set before themselves. It is about doing all that a leader can do to drive their vision and not getting distracted by irrelevant tasks or responsibilities. Stamina and tenacity play a vital role in the manifestation of this critical leadership competency. Leaders have to be resilient when facing challenges. When leaders fail to stay focused on their main objectives, endurance wanes. They get distracted and typically do not run the race that was set before them.

Compassion is about how we impact others. It is about taking time to get to know your people and truly understanding their strengths and development opportunities. It is about relational intelligence and empathy. When a leader takes time to build sustainable relationships with their people, they strengthen levels of commitment and accountability. Lastly, compassionate leadership is about courtesy. It is about doing unto others the things we would like them to do to us. Leaders who understand the importance of compassion have the greatest impact on people.

Inspiration builds off the momentum leaders create from compassion. When leaders genuinely take the time to build relationships with others, they open the door to influence and motivation. Inspiration is about giving people something to believe in. It is about having the rallying cry. It is about modeling a positive and passion-filled attitude for others to follow. Some of the most charismatic leaders I've worked with inspire at the individual and group level. They know how to sit one-on-one with people and get them to exceed expectations. At the same time, they can stand up in front of a packed auditorium and electrify an audience. Inspiration also takes courage. People are always watching those in leadership. How leaders handle setbacks inspires hope and helps people to strengthen and build character.

Innovation is about refining our goals and objectives along the way. We touched on goals in commitment and vigilance, but it is here that leaders make adjustments and course correct to get to their desired outcomes. Innovation is about trying different things and not being afraid to be creative when needed. It is about tracking progress against our vision and strategy. Leaders who do this best regularly partner with a coach or trusted advisor to monitor how they are doing. Leaders who run into trouble here typically are not willing to track progress and get easily distracted by competing priorities.

We wrap up our competencies with wisdom. Wisdom is about understanding the connectedness of life. It is about knowing how today's decisions will impact tomorrow. It is about discernment and intentionally surrounding yourself with wise people. Leaders who practice wisdom learn from experience. They remain open and aware of how different events impact their life. They understand how to grow from both positive and negative experiences. Additionally, they look for people who excel in the areas where they want to grow. They are not afraid to look for mentors and coaches to help them along the way. Lastly, leaders who exercise wisdom are lifelong learners. They understand that acquiring wisdom takes time and does not happen overnight. They keep the focus on learning and try to take something away from every experience that crosses their path.

It is my hope that this book will help you improve your own personal leadership style. Each chapter focuses on one of the ten leadership competencies. Every chapter begins with a quote about the competency that will hopefully get you thinking and reflecting on that behavior for your own leadership. Next, I will share a story from my consulting experiences about the competency. Names and organizations will be changed for confidentiality and to protect the clients I have worked with. From there, we will take a deep dive on the leadership competency and finish with guided recommendations on how you can grow in that area of leadership.

Leadership takes focus and commitment. It does not happen overnight. If you want to be a great leader, you need to practice these behaviors and take daily steps to improve. I've coached hundreds of clients over my career, and the ones who have made the largest and greatest strides are those who practice the things that will make them better leaders. My hope for you is that you can do the same. Remember, leadership is about impact. It is about helping people reach their full potential. At the end of the day, it is my belief that the growth and development of people is the highest calling of leadership. Good luck on your journey.

VISION

Vision without action is merely a dream. Action without vision just passes the time. Vision with action can change the world.

—Joel A. Barker

Jennifer was not your typical retail executive. She spent close to a decade working her way up through the organization at a time when men predominately got the promotions and key leadership roles. She was a fighter. Scrappy and driven, she did what was necessary to elevate her brand and leadership. I met Jennifer shortly after she was promoted to an SVP and region lead for the Northeast of a Fortune 100 retailer. She was three months into her role when I received a call. The conversation went something like this:

JENNIFER. Hello, Adam, I was given your name from one of our corporate HRBPs. I am having a lot of problems with one of my district managers, and we need you to do a 360 assessment and some coaching.

ADAM. I see. Can you tell me a little more about what has been going on with your district manager?

JENNIFER. Well, Ted has been with the company for over fifteen years. He has been successful in each of his last three roles but is beginning to get the reputation for leading with an iron fist. He does little to support his people and does not lead with a development mind-set. His people are afraid of him and worried when he visits their stores.

ADAM. Jennifer, I would be happy to help. Let's find some time to meet face-to-face so I can take you through our process and outline how I might be able to help Ted with some executive coaching.

Two weeks later, I met Jennifer for the first time. We were scheduled to meet for thirty minutes and talk primarily about Ted. From the moment we started the conversation, there was an immediate professional connection—the kind coaches dream of having with their clients, the kind that clients have when they find a true trusted advisor. We spent about fifteen to twenty minutes talking about the situation with Ted and the next two and half hours about Jennifer's leadership. She was stepping into a huge role and needed help motivating and galvanizing her team. This was a team of seventeen direct reports, most of which had very close relationships with one another and her predecessor. She was stepping out of his shadow and needed to build a vision for what her leadership team would look like, for what they would hope to accomplish collectively moving forward.

I knew Jennifer had to start with her personal vision. What did she want this role to be about? What impact did she want to leave on the organization? How could this filter down into the vision she would set for her team? We scheduled a half-day session to begin discussing her vision. Jennifer and I met in a conference room at the Grand Hyatt in Philadelphia at 8:00 a.m. We had to have some idea of what she wanted to share with her team in a three-day off-site that was to begin at 3:00 p.m. that day. We started talking about her leadership style. What had gotten her to this position? What did she value about people? How did she lead? How did she want to lead moving forward?

After about two hours of discussion, we started coming together with several areas she wanted for the region's vision. Her company is notorious for using acronyms, so we started taking her areas and looking for a word that could capture all of them. After some deliberation, we came up with something like M.O.T.I.V.A.T.E. Each letter represented one part of her vision for the team. For example, the *M* was for "meeting performance goals," *O* was for "outstanding customer service," *T* was for "teamwork," and so on. Jennifer was beginning to see how her personal vision for excellence could be translated into definable and measurable behaviors that she could share with her team.

I will never forget the experience when she unveiled the acronym and each behavior to the team. She shared the outline of the vision with great pride and confidence. This was something she put all her heart into. The other thing that was remarkable is she didn't talk at her team about the vision. She shared her initial ideas and then solicited feedback from all her direct reports. This process resonated with her team. They discussed the behaviors. The debated the areas of focus. They made changes to reflect everyone's thinking. At the end of the day, Jennifer and her team had a vision that they agreed upon for the region. They felt that they had collectively put in place the foundation for how they would lead the region over the next several years.

Jennifer understood the power of vision. She believed that it was the cornerstone for how her team would drive results and hold people accountable to desired expectations. She took the time to get clear for herself and then brought her people along to create their future. I was proud of her, and her team, for starting that journey together.

The Importance of Vision

Clients always ask me about goals and goal setting. How can we maximize performance? How can I get the best out of my people? What can we do to grow in the future? My answer is always simple: first, get clear about what you want the end state to look like. Set the vision for how you want things to play out and how you want to lead. Vision takes time and effort. The more work that is put in upfront to clearly outline the path forward, the greater the impact will be on others. With clarity comes commitment to a purpose, commitment to a mission.

When leaders do not start with setting a clear vision, challenges often arise. I've seen many leaders with the best of intentions miss this step and end up having trouble motivating and inspiring people later on. They also suffer from lack of focus and direction, which causes them to do too many things and not have a core purpose. When a strong vision is in the mix, people have a reason to go above and beyond current expectations. They have a desired end state that is worth moving toward. They put in the hard work and effort because they believe something great will take place if they remain focused on the key goals.

Vision is also tied to strategic planning in many instances. A solid vision lays the foundation for the typical three- or five-year strategic plan. For example, I once worked with a new CEO for a large technology company who had been selected by the board to come in and turn the company around. They had a track record of positive results and a solid product development history, but shareholders wanted new and innovative products out on the market to drive greater revenues and profits. This leader was succeeding the company's founder who was hesitant to take major risks and had instilled a conservative value system with his direct report team.

The first thing my client did when he arrived was to spend time with leaders from all levels of the organization. He wanted to a deeper understanding of the company's culture. He met with line-level managers in the manufacturing facilities. He held focus groups with sales and marketing leaders. He held town halls with research and product development people. After about three months of meeting with people and discussing the current state of the business, he met with the senior team and laid out his vision for the future. He wanted the company to be the leader in their product area and be known for the development of innovative and state-of-the-art products. This was a drastic change from the status quo these leaders were used to for so many years. However, as soon as the team bought into the vision, the path was set for developing three to five core strategic goals that they could look to attain over the next several years. These strategic outcomes ranged from capturing greater market share in their product categories to international expansion, to the development of several new product lines. Each of these strategic imperatives could be linked back to the vision. This gave the senior team purpose and a mission. It allowed them to get clear in their lines of business and how their teams could contribute to the desired outcomes.

Vision is also linked to problem-solving and critical-thinking skills. For years, psychologists have studied the links between intelligence and job performance. The findings indicate that higher levels of general intelligence lead to greater work outcomes. The same applies to vision setting. Leaders with greater intellectual horsepower think broader and deeper. They are able to connect the dots and think systemically about multiple issues. Some of the greatest visionary thinkers I have had the pleasure of working with were some of the brightest minds. They tend to operate at a high level, and they can process information quickly. This enables them to chart out issues two, three, or five years out. It helps them to look at issues from multiple angles.

One of my clients who was great at setting vision was probably one of the sharpest leaders I have ever worked with. He knew how to look at a problem and dissect it in many different ways. When I first began working with him, we were tasked with developing a three-year strategy plan for his organization. The company had been through some challenging times, and they were losing market share to many of their competitors. I remember sitting with him and talking through the issues. He started mapping out the competitive landscape, recent consumer trends, macro issues impacting consumer spending in the economy, and so forth. I was amazed at how he was able to string together all the issues and bring it back to identifying the best path forward for his organization.

We started with identifying the ideal future state for his organization. He knew there were three key priorities that would drive the business, but he first had to get clear on the overarching objective. With some discussion, he came to the conclusion that his vision was to be the number one consumer products company in the industry. From this vision, we discussed the key strategic objectives that would need to be accomplished in order to make the vision a reality. First, he need manufacturing to revamp their facilities across the organization. Next, he needed to expand operations internationally to grow the company's global footprint. Lastly, they needed to upgrade the entire IT infrastructure to support the corporate functions across all levels of the organization. With these three key objectives tied to his vision, he was ready to engage his senior team and make sure to get their input and perspectives.

We met with the team on a cold October day. Each functional leader had their own priorities for the following year, and it was my client's objective to get them all aligned and motivated to pursue the key objectives that would bring his vision to life. We started by letting each leader share one key objective they hoped to attain the following year. Then my client shared his vision and strategic priorities for the future and how each of their objectives could be tied into the vision. As they talked through the key issues, I could see the alignment and agreement begin to take place. There were some debates and some slight changes made to his top three areas, but we finished the day with the team rallying behind his vision. My client understood the value of vision. He used his analytical and critical thinking skills to survey the landscape and process the information needed to chart a course for his team. This helped them pursue their key objectives and allowed the organization to have a plan moving forward.

Action Steps for Leading with Vision

Build your playbook

Making your vision become a reality takes time and effort. Building a playbook for how you intend to get to your desired outcome is key. Leaders who develop a strong playbook have a game plan for their teams to follow. Without a playbook, leaders may have an overarching goal they're attempting to achieve but won't get there, given the lack of focus and disciplined detail concerning their plan. Many of my clients come to me for support on developing their playbook. What areas should they focus on? What trade-offs should be made? Who should be involved and where should they put forth effort? These are just some of the questions that need to be answered as you map out your playbook.

The first critical component of the playbook is identifying three to five key objectives that people can work to make the vision a reality. I once worked with the president of a medical devices company, and we focused on several areas for his organization. The vision was simple: be the best medical device provider in their market. From this vision, we outlined key priorities for the business. There was the focus on R&D and product development. There was the refinement of training for the sales force. There was a campaign to improve their marketing efforts. There was greater emphasis placed on recruitment and selection of top talent. And there was a commitment to developing the capabilities of their high-potential leaders. The combination of these areas provided clear guidelines for each function leader. From here, each functional head could build their individual plan for making the goal a reality.

The second priority is ensuring that the objectives identified are things that people buy into. We will touch on bringing others along in a moment, but for now, it is important to ensure the playbook objectives cover different areas of the business. Make sure to think through critical strategic issues such as where your business is headed in the next two to three years? Who are the top competitors in your industry? How can you beat them in the marketplace? How are your clients and/or customers changing? What are the trends taking place in the broader economy? How should your business continue to evolve and stay on the cutting edge of whatever product or service you deliver?

Lastly, it is important to make sure the key strategic priorities are directly linked to your vision. They have to be realistic and practical. For example, if your business has never developed products in a particular category, you shouldn't set a goal to be the leading provider in the industry. Make sure the key priorities can be attained with disciplined, concerted effort. Setting objectives that are too grandiose or difficult for people to attain will cause your people and organization to burn out quickly.

Bring others along

No leader can scale the mountain all by themselves. We need others. We need capable and skilled people around us who can help make the vision a reality. Some of the best leaders I have worked with surrounded themselves with people who complement their strengths. They have the inner confidence and courage to select team members who have strengths in different areas of expertise, areas that they know will be needed to bring the vision into focus. When we surround ourselves with talented counterparts and collectively build the vision together, great things can begin to happen. People take pride in going above and beyond their current work rhythms to bring the vision to pass. Colleagues feel more committed to the vision if they have a say in helping to shape the key objectives. Team members want to work together collaboratively when they realize that their individual efforts are serving a greater good.

To bring others along, there are four things that are important to implement. First, you need to select team members and colleagues who have strengths where you have weaknesses. Do not be afraid that they might outshine you in a particular area. This should happen if you select the best talent. For example, if the vision is to be the number one consumer products company in the world, then make sure you get the best product development leaders, the best marketing and sales leaders, the best manufacturing and operations leaders, and so forth.

Next, it is important to include your team members in the early stages of vision setting. This was the most important thing that Jennifer did. As soon as she had an idea of what the vision was going to be, she brought her team together to share the idea. Not only did she share the ideas, but she solicited input and feedback from them in shaping the vision. It made the vision better than she ever could have done on her own. The more you can bring bright and strategic minds to the mix, the better the outcome will be.

Third, it is important to include people as part of your thinking and planning as things evolve. No vision is perfect from its inception. Things have to evolve over time as many factors (e.g., external environment, demands on the business, customer trends) change. Make sure the vision is discussed regularly so people can make adjustments and changes to their part of the vision as needed. Remember this ancient proverb "Without counsel, plans go awry, but in the multitude of advisors, they are established upon a solid foundation."

Lastly, it is important to allow your team to have constructive discussions and debate about the vision along the way. You have to calibrate along the journey if a vision is to become a reality. Some of the best leaders take time each quarter to bring their senior teams together. They check in on the overarching vision and each of the key priorities for their people. If things need to change, make sure you are willing to make the necessary adjustments. And do not be afraid if people want to modify their specific objectives in service of the vision. Flexibility is key here. We will discuss more of this in the chapter on innovation. For now, it is important to understand that evolution takes collaboration, and a willingness to change what is needed.

Celebrate the victories

Life moves quickly. As leaders, there is always the next milestone to achieve, the next mountain to climb. If leaders aren't careful, they can lose sight of the present and miss out on opportunities to encourage and support their team. I've seen many leaders who constantly push and strive for the next accomplishment. This leads to burnout with their teams because there wasn't time taken to slow down and celebrate.

Jennifer understood the need to celebrate just as much as she understood the need to set a vision for her team. Her company operated with a "work hard, play hard" mentality. This was important because it gave her people time to celebrate. Twice a year, she would bring all her district and store managers together for a strategic leadership meeting. There were probably five hundred to six hundred people invited to these meetings. They were inspirational. The two to three days would focus on taking stock of the current environment and progress toward goals. They would also celebrate people's successes and take time to refocus their efforts. I saw leaders leave this meeting energized and committed to moving the vision forward for the business.

I've also seen a few leaders push and push without taking the time to celebrate the victories. One leader in particular was constantly fixated on the future. He lost sight of the present, and it had a negative effect on his people. His organization had high turnover, and people had low job satisfaction. It wasn't until he started to slow down and encourage people through praise and recognition that things started to turn around. It took some time, but he was able to learn the behaviors that were necessary for motivating and celebrating with his people. So remember to celebrate the successes that you and others have along the way. Tell your people how proud you are of their accomplishments. Do this, and they will stick with you through thick and thin.

For a leader, vision is everything. However, once the vision is set, it is important to build a playbook, bring people along the journey, and celebrate your team's success. Practice these critical behaviors, and your team will drive long-term sustainable success. You will also have people who want to remain aligned and focused on making the vision a reality.

PASSION

Light yourself on fire with passion, and people
will come from miles to watch you burn.

—John Wesley

Ivan was born with a fire in the belly. Of Spanish descent, he moved
to the United States at the age of eleven. He knew little about American
culture at the time but was inspired by the American Dream and all
it could mean for his future. He tirelessly worked his way up through
high school and college before moving into the healthcare industry.
Labeled as a high potential early in his career, Ivan thrived under pressure and competition. He loved the thrill of the sale and building a
new customer base.

As a natural people person, he was quick to establish rapport
with others and build strong, sustainable relationships. People also
valued his honesty and integrity. Ivan did not cut corners, nor did
he take shortcuts to get to his desired outcomes. He put in the hard
work and effort, tireless effort at times, to make things happen.
Through his diligence and determination, he moved from sales rep
to manager, from manager to regional leader, from regional leader to
director, and from director to vice president.

I met Ivan about ten years into his career, as he was looking to
make a job transition from a larger health care provider to a smaller
company. From the instant we met, we had strong rapport. We are
both fans of the Miami Heat, so there was a lot to talk about, especially during the Lebron James and Dwayne Wade era. I assessed
Ivan for a vice president role overseeing the Southern Europe region.
Throughout the executive assessment interview, his drive, high
energy, and passion resonated with me tremendously. Within five

minutes of sitting with Ivan, anyone could tell how motivated and inspired he was to succeed. He was determined to make his life and career all about accomplishment. I thought he would be a great fit for the role and the organization. I made my recommendation to the hiring leader and suggested onboarding coaching.

Ivan was offered the role, and shortly thereafter, I began his executive integration coaching. We ended up working together for a year and a half, and I can honestly say I have never seen another executive with more passion and drive than Ivan. We sometimes joked that he never slept! He would always be on a plane heading to one of the nine countries under his leadership. He would do whatever was necessary to win. This resonated with his people. They were excited about the prospects for the future and quickly followed his lead.

My most memorable experience with Ivan was when he invited me to present at his annual all-employee sales meeting in Monte Carlo. I watched as he gave a rousing speech to over a thousand employees. He outlined their goals and objectives for the year while celebrating the things they had achieved the year before. You could tell all of his employees were committed to the overarching mission and vision for Southern Europe. Ivan rallied his troops behind a compelling and inspiring future state. As any organization would, they had challenges along the way, but Ivan never gave up that passion and intensity. He believed in his heart of hearts that they could be better. He pushed his team to strive for excellence.

Today, Ivan is a group president of a medical devices business. He has hopes and dreams of becoming a CEO one day. I see this in his future. His passion, energy, enthusiasm, and desire to win are contagious. Pair this with his intellectual horsepower, strategic capabilities, and focus on execution; and it's no wonder he had become a success story. Ivan understood the importance of bringing passion to his leadership. Without it, people lack commitment and the fortitude to succeed. He leveraged this competency to build buy-in, focus, and commitment from his team and the broader organization. I am delighted to have coached him during his early career and see him accomplish his goals and objectives. The future is bright for

Ivan. Passion is the key ingredient that helped him accomplish his dreams.

The Importance of Passion

Passion breeds commitment. It breeds disciplined effort and the burning desire to do all that is necessary to win. I've seen many leaders use passion to impact the people around them. When they bring energy and excitement to their work, it is contagious. People want to perform better and give their all. I remember one client I worked with in the manufacturing industry. This leader always had a smile on his face and took time to recognize people for their efforts. It wasn't anything major but just a "Thank you" here, "Great job" there; and people wanted to deliver for this leader. He would also take time to share his hopes and dreams for the organization and the business with people at any chance he could get. This made people feel that their day-to-day responsibilities had meaning. They were connected to something greater than their individual output.

I've also seen situations where leaders have not instilled passion and enthusiasm in the workplace. In these instances, people dread coming to work. There is no camaraderie or rallying cry that people get behind. They slowly do their work to get through the day and are not committed to the mission. I once worked with an executive who was going through some personal issues with his family. Although people say to keep work and family separate, in reality, it is hard to do this consistently. The issues at home inevitably come to work and vice versa. Given his issues on the home front, he was distracted and did not bring the passion and drive needed to inspire his employees. They picked up on his low energy and lack of vitality quickly. It sent a current of negative energy throughout the organization. This lasted for several months and ultimately cost them millions of dollars in sales due to a lack of motivation and poor performance. Without passion, people will come up with all types of excuses as to why they struggle with focus and effort. Passion is the fuel that keeps the fires of performance burning.

The Link between Passion and Positive Psychology

Passion in the workplace has its origins in the field of positive psychology. For the last forty years, this field has contributed a wealth of research and information about passion, happiness, and fulfillment. Martin Seligman, the father and pioneer of positive psychology, believed that the most satisfied, upbeat people were those who had discovered and exploited their unique combination of "signature strengths," such as humanity, temperance, and persistence.

Seligman viewed happiness and the pursuit of our passions in three categories: (a) the Pleasant Life—learning to savor and appreciate basic pleasures such as companionship; (b) the Good Life—achieved through discovering our unique virtues and strengths and employing them with passion and energy to enhance our lives; and (c) the Meaningful Life—finding a deep sense of fulfillment by using our unique strengths for a purpose greater than ourselves. All three of these areas can be applied to our work lives and can be enhanced by injecting energy and passion into what we believe we are called to do.

We will start with the Pleasant Life. In organizations, I have seen this manifest itself in many different ways. The most common is in the relationships coworkers develop with one another. Some of my best clients have developed organizational cultures where camaraderie and collaboration are the norm. In these environments, people trust one another, they work collaboratively to achieve shared goals, and they celebrate victories as a team. One of my clients in particular believed relationship building was so critical to the company's success that it was the number one leadership competency they instilled in their people. I saw executives and senior leaders go out of their way to engage new employees in order to help onboard and integrate them into the culture. This reinforced the belief that nothing can be accomplished without strong relationships and teamwork.

The Pleasant Life also manifests itself in one of the most important work relationships. That is the relationship between manager and direct report. This is where mentoring, coaching, and feedback become so critical to people's success. Leaders who partner with their direct reports instill a sense of passion from them. Specifically, when a leader takes time to give feedback and coach a direct report, this strengthens their professional bond. It allows the direct report to grow faster and take on greater areas of responsibility. I saw this in my own career with the first management consulting firm I joined over twenty years ago. My manager knew that I was green and right out of graduate school. He took the time to help me cultivate a strong foundation around consulting and how to deliver the services that our firm specialized in. I witnessed him develop business with a passionate and entrepreneurial mind-set. I sat in on meetings with a number of his clients and saw how he interacted with them—how he built trust, offered perspective, and guided people toward improvements in their leadership. This helped accelerate my growth. Our relationship grew over my first few years with the firm. My performance skyrocketed because of his concerted effort to see me develop and grow. I brought a degree of passion and enthusiasm to my work based on what I saw him do day in and day out.

Passion is found in the Good Life through the identification of our key strengths and virtues. Once we understand what it is that we are good at, we can deploy these skills in ways that energize and enhance our lives. It is amazing to see leaders accelerate their growth and performance once they truly identify what their strengths are. I've worked with hundreds of leaders who got clear about their major strengths and were able to leverage these capabilities to maximize performance.

Some of the most memorable examples involved leaders who leveraged an assessment process as part of their development. The executive assessment process is a great tool for helping leaders figure out their core strengths. Through the use of psychological testing (e.g., leadership competencies, personality characteristics, and intellectual horsepower), 360-degree feedback, and in-depth interviews, leaders can gain tremendous insight into their key strengths. Once they understand these areas, they can focus on them and begin to delegate the things that do not fall into their wheelhouse. It takes time and commitment, but the leaders who identify and leverage their strengths are typically the most engaging, energetic, and passionate leaders. This occurs because they get laser clear about what they do well and where to deploy their skills.

Another component of the Good Life is understanding one's areas of opportunity. Almost as important as identifying strengths, getting clear on development areas allows a leader to do several things. First, it helps them to recruit and retain talent in areas where they might struggle. The best teams have members who complement each other. The leader has a certain skill set, and all his direct reports bring unique talent and capabilities to the mix. Second, it allows leaders to work on their gaps through coaching and development. I believe leaders should spend most of their time focused on their strengths. However, there are instances where knowing, and working on, one's development opportunities is beneficial to a leader's professional growth.

Lastly, through the identification of one's development opportunities, a leader can determine if other members of their team share similar gaps. If this is the case, the team can work on collective goals to improve their performance. I've worked with many teams that share similar areas of opportunity such as being more strategic, delegating responsibilities, focusing on innovation, streamlining processes and procedures, and speeding execution. When the team knows that one particular area is impacting many parts of the organization, they can focus resources on addressing the issue, doing so with passion.

The Meaningful Life is all about legacy and purpose. It is about finding a deep sense of fulfillment in what we do and linking our skill sets to a purpose that is greater than ourselves. My clients typically like to talk about leadership legacy, and this is where the Meaningful Life comes into play. I will often ask clients, "What is the mark you want to leave with others when you retire or leave this role?" I get many different responses to that question, but some of the common ones include "I want to leave the business or organization better than it was when I took on this role," "I want to help my people grow and promote them into roles of greater responsibility and scope," and "I want to help us become the best provider in our industry sector." All of these responses have to do with purpose. They are about striving to impact people and the business long after we're gone. The best leaders understand the value of meaning and purpose. They know how to link it to their vision, and it keeps them committed to ongoing growth and development.

Action Steps for Leading with Passion

Follow your heart

The best leaders identify the things that truly get them energized and excited. For some, it is seeing the people around them grow and develop. I once worked with an executive who prided himself on hiring and developing the best people. He would regularly take time for coaching, feedback, and mentoring. People grew tremendously because this leader took the time to develop their capabilities. I asked him once why he valued that so much. His response was simple. He had a mentor early on in his career, and it helped his growth; it enabled him to have the confidence required to pursue his dreams.

Other leaders believe in getting involved and hands-on in the work. They do not look at hierarchy as some corporate organizational design. They enjoy rolling their sleeves up and being out in the field or in the lab with their teams. These leaders are typically your teachers. Their passion is in doing the work and educating their folks along the way. They lead by example and strive to put in just as much, if not more, work and effort as their people. These leaders value impact and look to demonstrate this to all they come into contact with.

Some leaders like to lead from afar. Hierarchy is important to them. Their passions revolve around managing processes and procedures in overseeing and guiding the work of their people. The strongest leaders in this area respect the people who have come before them. They understand and internalize the formal rules of engagement in organizations and look to direct the actions and activities of others. I often find these types of leaders to be keenly aware of how their teams are performing, not because they get directly involved in the work on a daily basis, but because they keep a close watch on their people and leverage the relationships that they have built with their direct reports.

Whatever it is that you enjoy doing deep down at your core, make sure you are doing it. Leaders often run into problems when they try to do too much, when they try to be all things to all people. This is one of the biggest challenges for new leaders—moving from execution to influence. As their roles get larger, the need for clarity of purpose becomes greater. By following their heart's desire, they are able to lead with passion in a way that has a positive impact on others. People easily follow their lead.

Identify and leverage your strengths

Once you have found the things that mean the most to you, it is important to get crystal clear about what you do well. You may like to influence others but have never been in a role or situation where you have had to do so without authority. You enjoy thinking strategically, and big picture, but have spent most of your career to date focusing on execution and driving results. You need to determine what your key strengths are.

Most leaders have two or three things that they do exceptionally well. Work with a coach or a mentor to verify the things you believe are virtues are actual strengths in the eyes of colleagues. The best way to get clear about your assets is through the process of 360-degree feedback. This process enables leaders to get a sense of their strengths and opportunities from a cross-section of colleagues across the organization. A good 360-degree process will solicit input from managers, peers, direct reports, cross-functional colleagues, and external stakeholders. I've seen many leaders leverage the 360-degree feedback process to determine their strengths and then take action to leverage these capabilities. Once strengths have been identified, I believe it is essential to spend 80 to 90 percent of your time focused on what you do well. There is a time and place to focus on your development opportunities, but when it comes to leading with passion, you have to stick to what will drive success for your business.

By focusing on your strengths, you will give the greatest effort and energy to delivering outstanding results. The reason behind this is that we do our best when we are focused on the areas where we perform the strongest. Let others focus on the areas where you have developmental opportunities. Some of the best leaders understand what their gaps are and know how to hand things off to others. Humility plays a big part here as few leaders wants to admit they have gaps; however, the ones who can check their ego usually bring on people with exceptional strengths and trust them to deliver. One of the best CEOs I have ever worked with understood the importance of surrounding himself with stellar performers and making sure to let them lead in the areas of his weaknesses. He was great at setting vision and inspiring others but was not one for detail and regularly managing the process. After going through a 360-degree feedback process and understanding this, he quickly brought in a COO who was very hands-on and detailed oriented. This helped increase productivity and allowed the CEO to focus on what he did best. They complemented each other in a great way.

Link your passions to mission and purpose

Our passions lead to our purpose as leaders. In consulting with my clients, I often ask them some of the following questions to get at mission and purpose: What is the impact you want to leave on your people and the organization? Who do you want to inspire and motivate? Who do you want to leave a lasting legacy with? What do you want to have been known for after you retire? These questions spark the inner drive and motivation to be more and contribute more beyond the day-to-day. When our passions, the things that we do well, are linked to an overarching mission and purpose, the real juice of life starts to manifest itself.

One of my clients really took this idea to heart a few years back. He had stepped in as a new CEO for a Fortune 500 company and really wanted to make a lasting impact. It was not good enough for him to be successful in his role; he wanted to leave the company in a much better state than when he first stepped into the role. We embarked on the journey of making this a reality. First, we identified what was most important to him. He was an innovator at heart. He loved to brainstorm ideas and develop products that would change his industry fifteen to twenty years into the future. Once we determined what was most important, we moved to understanding and leveraging his strengths. He was strategic and big picture in his thinking. He understood how to sell others on an idea and mobilize people to action. He had an unwavering work ethic that inspired the people around him. We leveraged these strengths to spark the vision and strategic outlook for the organization.

We then began to map out how his product innovations would shape the industry over the next decade. He brought his people along for this journey and got all of his R&D and manufacturing leaders aligned around the path they were to take forward. I never saw someone cultivate greater buy-in and commitment from people. His team understood the mission and what they were trying to accomplish collectively. This leader understood his true calling and did not let anything get in the way of his ability to accomplish his goals. It took time, effort, and hard work; but he never gave up on his purpose and calling as a leader.

I've also had the unfortunate experience of working with leaders who have difficulty linking passion to purpose. One leader in particular tried to be a jack of all trades. He had trouble delegating to his direct reports and always had to be at the center of all the action. His leadership style was more hub-and-spoke, which made everyone dependent on him to accomplish their responsibilities. This slowed processes down and prevented his team from maximizing their full potential. This leader also had difficulty accepting feedback and felt he had strengths in many different areas. This caused him to focus on way too many things and not get clear on his key strengths and capabilities. When leaders do this, it becomes hard to inspire others. You have to show vulnerability and a willingness to let things go if you want people to follow your lead. This leader struggled with this, and it cost his organization a lot in the long-term.

Be willing to make sacrifices

Passion at its truest essence is about sacrifice. As leaders, we tend to give our all when we truly believe in what we're doing, when we truly value and love our work. This inevitably requires dedication and sacrifice. Leaders need to sacrifice for other people. They need to set an example and at times sacrifice their personal interests for the greater good. Some of the most talented leaders I have worked with understand this principle. They look for opportunities to make an impact and show others how their passion is displayed on a consistent basis.

One of the more memorable consulting experiences I have had was with a leader who went to great lengths to make sacrifices for his people and organization. When I met this leader, he had just gone through a major merger and acquisition. His company had acquired one of the largest consumer products companies in the US, and it was his job as CEO to merge the two cultures. This was not going to be an easy task by any stretch of the imagination. For years, the two companies had been major competitors, and this filtered down to the employee level. At first, people from the two companies did not want to be in the same room with one another, let alone work together. My client had to set the tone from the top and make tough decisions to show both organizations that they could thrive collectively as one organization.

We started with his vision for the combined enterprise. What did he want the new organization to stand for? How did he want his employees to interact with one another? What was going to be the new rallying cry? How was he going to merge the two distinct cultures? These were not easy questions to answer. It took time and disciplined effort to focus on each area and take the necessary time to make sure he got things right. This took tremendous sacrifice on his part. There were many early days and late nights. He set the tone for his leadership team and worked tirelessly to ensure the merger was successful. Although he was willing to put the time and effort in, there were definitely bumps in the road along the journey.

One issue was determining who would be fit for specific roles and take on new leadership positions in the combined organization. He was committed to doing a thorough assessment of every leader's capabilities to determine the best fit. This is where my firm came into the mix as we conducted development assessments for close to one hundred executives. We helped them get clear on what good leadership (i.e., the critical leadership competencies in the new organization) would look like and then assessed all the leaders against this framework. It was his passion for excellence and focus on getting the right leaders in the right roles that enabled his people to buy in to this idea and take it on with the right spirit.

Another issue involved setting the right cultural tone for the combined organization. My client did not want to simply integrate the acquired company and keep all of the norms, values, and beliefs from his organization. He was interested in taking the best from both companies and making a bright collective future. I was impressed by the sacrifices he made to make this come to life. He worked tirelessly with his leadership team and leaders from the acquired company to ensure the right operating environment and organizational culture was put in place. In the long run, the acquisition and its integration was successful because of his fortitude and willingness to make the necessary sacrifices to create a strong, unified organization.

Passion drives success. It enables leaders to bring forth the energy and enthusiasm that is needed to make dreams a reality. Leaders who are passionate create a climate where people are empowered to make decisions and challenge the status quo. They talk beyond today and anticipate new possibilities for the team and organization. They see possibilities and make them happen. If you want to lead with passion, make sure to focus on operating with a never-ending desire to be the best in your area of expertise. Be proactive in seizing opportunities and fully engaged in your work. This will enable you to manage resistance and fear of change at all levels with openness, clarity, and objectivity.

COMMITMENT

There's a difference between interest and commitment.
When you're interested in doing something, you do it
only when it's convenient. When you're committed to
something, you accept no excuses, only results.
—Kenneth Blanchard

The financial crisis of 2008 hit many US companies hard. The economic landscape was hit the worse in the finance and insurance sector. Many companies collapsed and had to close their doors. Luckily, my client's company was given an opportunity to rebound and rebuild. Although they were given the chance to turn things around, Candace, their CEO, had a tall order in front of her. She needed to restructure and redesign the entire organization and make sure the right leaders were in the right roles to get through the turnaround. It was around this time that Candace reached out to my firm to inquire about our process for leadership development assessments. She had gone through a leadership development process earlier in her career and thought it would be important to give her top thirty leaders the insights they needed to make the changes required for future success.

When we first met with Candace, she had a specific framework in mind for how she wanted the assessment process to go. We would need to build a leadership competency model that would reflect where the company was headed—its future state, and not the current circumstances. She wanted leaders to be open about their reports and feedback and use this process as a mechanism for driving the changes needed at all levels of the organization. She was fully committed to seeing this development process through from start to finish. Based on her request, my firm crafted a series of assessment protocols to get her people the input and feedback they needed. We used a multimethod assessment approach involving a three-hour in-depth leadership interview, critical thinking tests and leadership personality instruments, interview-based 360-degree feedback, and external résumé benchmarking and job profiling. The combination of these assessment tools enabled us to get accurate and detailed information about their leaders. We then used this data to compare each leader to the leadership competency framework we developed for the future state of the organization.

From start to finish, the assessment and feedback process took close to eight months. It was by no means a smooth process. Many of her top leaders did not feel the need for a leadership assessment at such a pivotal junction in the company's history. Others did not want to go through a 360-degree feedback process and definitely did not want to share the results of the assessment with Candace or one another. Despite these obstacles, Candace remained steadfast and determined to have her entire leadership team go through the assessment and feedback process. She felt it was critical to their growth and ability to effectively lead toward the future. Candace understood the importance of commitment. She had the fortitude to stay the course and make tough decisions for the benefits of the enterprise. She made sure that her team persevered through this process despite operating in a high-stress and complex economic environment.

Feedback can do many things to a leader. They will either reject the assessment or get very defensive with a consultant. This is not a strong starting point for behavior change. In other instances, the light goes off, and leaders take the feedback to heart. They use it to make improvements and strive to be better. Luckily for my firm, once all the leaders received their feedback, many of them responded positively. They found the exercise and the insights and feedback derived from the process to be immensely helpful. It enabled them to look at their personal impact and that of their teams. It built a sense of trust and camaraderie between leaders as they began to restructure and redesign the organization. It created the environment for a strong rebound and rebuilding of the company post the economic crisis.

Not only was the feedback process helpful to Candace and her top thirty leaders, but it initiated a focus on leadership and organizational effectiveness throughout their company. Once the top thirty leaders were given feedback, they wanted to offer this opportunity for many of their direct reports. We began working to drive positive leadership change across various areas of the business. Additionally, through Candace's commitment to driving true leadership impact and change, the organization partnered with my firm to design key leadership competencies that would have an impact across functional boundaries and at various levels of leadership. We took the leadership framework that was used for the top thirty leadership assessments and cascaded this down to the SVP, VP, and director levels. As time progressed, we began to see the leadership changes start to take place across the business. Leaders at all levels were more open to feedback from one another and from external stakeholders. Teams began focusing on their collective effectiveness. HR leaders began partnering with us to design a talent development program that would prepare high potentials for future roles of increased responsibility and scope. We were witnessing a true leadership turnaround, and it all began with Candace's commitment to excellence in her people's leadership.

Candace understood the importance of commitment. She knew how to strive for a critical goal despite obstacles and setbacks. She challenged her people to be greater and invited them to take part in the story of evolution and change. She prioritized leadership effectiveness as a critical growth factor to get her organization through the turnaround. This fostered clarity of purpose for her people and helped them navigate times of doubt and uncertainty. Candace persisted despite the circumstances. She had the necessary focus and concentration to push her team through a difficult period and achieve their desired outcomes.

The Impact of Commitment on Leadership Effectiveness

Commitment is about remaining steadfast and unwavering in our goals and objectives. Whether that is galvanizing a team to achieve a vision or staying focused on hitting a sales target, commitment is about never giving up on a desired outcome. The greatest leaders understand that commitment takes place on an individual, team, and organizational level. At the individual level, commitment is about keeping our word and delivering on our responsibilities. This can be accomplished by focusing on the critical few priorities that will drive results. In working with many new leaders, this can be one of the more challenging areas of growth. Those who are promoted into leadership roles have typically been strong individual contributors. Once they step into a leadership role, the need for delegation and balancing one's commitments becomes critical. Leaders who can focus on their key objectives and effectively hand work off to others typically accomplish their goals.

At the team level, commitment is about properly sequencing and socializing ideas and strategies that others can follow. The team leader needs to identify the key initiatives and create a sustainable work rhythm for their people. This involves proper resource allocation and ensuring the things that get prioritized have a material impact on the business. Team leaders also need to be comfortable with ambiguity and uncertainty. They have to demonstrate the fortitude to stay the course and make the tough decisions, despite obstacles and challenges. The strongest team leaders encourage their teams to pursue their objectives, and they invite input from others. They create viable feedback loops with key stakeholders to anticipate needs and track performance. They are also willing to make adjustments to vision and strategy based upon ongoing feedback from the business.

At the organizational level, commitment is about persisting in overcoming obstacles from a variety of internal and external sources— from other departments and business units, from customers and clients, and from important external stakeholders. It is about exerting the necessary concentration to handle turbulent economic periods and deploying sound judgment in prioritizing organizational objectives. As CEOs and senior executives, it is about emphasizing and reinforcing the importance of having a collective sense of mission and purpose. It is about staying committed to the vision or mission and consistently delivering a message of hope, passion, and excitement for the future. Additionally, when senior leaders can establish reporting processes and systems that are highly efficient and accurate, this allows for more energy to go to adding value to the organization. It allows people to focus on their responsibilities and leverage their strengths and capabilities to drive results.

Although commitment can impact an organization on many levels, I typically see senior leaders spend the most commitment on driving results; they are focused on anything that will grow the bottom line. Although this keeps the shareholders happy, it can sometimes impact one's leadership style. This is most noticeable when clients envision a larger leadership or talent development program and quickly scrap it a few months later if business is not performing well. This is a big mistake. Staying committed to developing people is just as important as commitment to financial objectives. The greatest leaders look to grow their people and are committed to ongoing professional development. People are the greatest asset of any organization, so investing in their growth is key to driving long-term success. It will ultimately impact the bottom line if it is seen through to the end.

Action Steps for Leading with Commitment

Reap what you sow

Commitment is all about reaping what you sow. You need to be diligent in your efforts and prepare for the unexpected. The interesting thing about sowing and reaping is that it can work for the positive or the negative. The principle is universal in its application. I've seen sowing and reaping have a tremendous positive impact on some of my clients' leadership effectiveness. I've also had the unfortunate experience of working with some derailing executives that have sowed discord, dishonesty, and chaos only to reap disaster in the end.

One leader I remember in particular applied this principle and wreaked havoc across his professional and personal life. This senior leader was skilled at compartmentalizing different things. He was also an excellent social chameleon—skilled at adjusting his style and personality to fit the moment. From the outside, this leader had it all—a high-level, well-paid SVP job in a manufacturing organization, a wonderful family and personal life, and strong personal relationships. Unfortunately, much of this began to crumble as he developed a substance abuse addiction over the course of several years. As a result of the addiction, he began to struggle immensely on the job front. He had difficulty keeping commitments to colleagues and customers. He had trouble getting to work and focusing on his responsibilities each day. On the personal front, his marriage was in shambles as he hid his addiction from his wife and loved ones. This terrible negative spiral went on for three years as he ended up losing his job and eventually lost his marriage. This leader had hit rock bottom due to sowing and reaping negativity across his life.

When I met with this leader, he had nothing left. You could see the defeat in his face. After losing everything he had worked for over his career, he needed help to begin the process of rebuilding his life. I started doing some pro bono coaching with him to get his professional life back on track. He had to start sowing positive things in all areas of his life if he was going to reap future success. The journey he was on was long, painful at times, and progressed slowly day-by-day. Despite all the challenges he faced, I admired his steadfast commitment to turning things around. On the personal front, he checked himself into a rehab facility and slowly got his mental and physical health back in order. On the professional front, we started identifying what he was most passionate about, the things that would give him the most joy and feelings of contribution. He had let go of his dreams for so many years, and now was the time to reignite his fire.

We identified the things that mattered most to his career and his future and then began putting things in place to make his new dreams a reality. The process took time, and he had to remain focused on the overarching objectives through the challenging and difficult periods. There were moments of fear and doubt, but he persisted through these periods. In the end, I witnessed my client make a complete turnaround in his work and personal life. He had been given a second chance at life, and I witnessed his devotion and commitment to seizing the moment and making the best of every situation.

As leaders, people will always eventually reap what they sow. Make sure to sow positivity and hope into the lives of others. Whether it is your direct reports, colleagues, customers, or other stakeholders, the process of sowing in people's lives reaps immense benefits. Similarly, sow goals and objectives into processes and procedures that will drive success. For example, if you have an idea for a product or service, do the legwork to plant the proper seeds that will bring your idea to life. Take time to research ideas and chart out a course to make your dreams a reality. Not only will this help you reap success, but it will also serve as a positive example for the people around you. Sowing and reaping always have an impact on people. When they see someone taking the time and effort to make something happen, the focus on commitment and dedication becomes infectious. It pushes people to remain determined in setting and achieving their own goals.

Be open to making adjustments

No plan is flawless from its inception. Developing ideas and charting a course for their attainment is important, but unforeseen challenges will inevitably arise. As leaders, people need to remain open to the changes that will occur in the pursuit of their goals. Leaders need to be flexible and willing to make adjustments as needed. Some of the strongest leaders whom I have worked with practice this behavior with their teams regularly. They will chart a course, provide direction to their team members, and then solicit input and feedback about progress being made along the way. They do not get frustrated by challenges and temporary setbacks. Instead, they adapt to the circumstances and remain focused on the long-term objective.

I once worked with a senior leader in the pharmaceutical industry who was skilled at making adjustments based on feedback from others. This leader believed that her people were the best resources to leverage with regards to how progress was being made against key objectives. She would meet with each of her direct reports on a monthly basis for status updates on each of their top priorities. As challenges and obstacles arose, she would partner with her people in problem-solving and refocusing efforts. She also believed in bringing her team together several times a year to conduct a pulse check on their main initiatives. I found her to be humble and open to input from her people. She had the drive and commitment to keep her team on task but did not have to have things done her way. If team members could identify better ways to get to desired outcomes, she supported their efforts. Through her leadership, the team met their goals for three consecutive years. It was her commitment to excellence that drove the team, but it was her flexibility and comfort with making adjustment that helped them navigate the challenging times.

I have also experienced working with leaders who are rigid and inflexible. They believe their ideas and their approach are the best way to achieve results. When this occurs, people become frustrated and lack the freedom to course correct over time. It also prevents teams from sharing feedback with one another and fostering a culture of learning. In many of these situations, I often see people become so frustrated that they end up quitting given the lack of willingness from their manager to make adjustments as obstacles arise. Typically, leaders who behave in this fashion do not stay in key roles for a long period of time. They tend to get demoted quickly given the inability to adapt to their circumstances.

Innovation and creativity are also important factors when it comes to making adjustments. Leaders have to be willing to modify their objectives and adapt to changing times. However, they do not have to come up with all the innovations and novel ideas on their own. This is where leveraging the skills and expertise of others comes in. If a leader has team members who have different points of view and can add sparks of creativity to processes or procedures, they should encourage people to share these perspectives. As in most things related to team effectiveness, it is the collective efforts and partnership that drives results. Leaders who understand this and are willing to take ideas from their people get to the best possible outcomes.

Conquer adversity

Related to making adjustments is the ability to persist through challenging periods and conquer adversity. In leadership, this can ultimately be the make-it-or-break-it factor for many people. It is easy to lead when times are good; when business is thriving, employees are satisfied, and objectives are being achieved. However, the real test of leadership is when adversity strikes. How people respond to hardships demonstrates their character and fortitude.

Over the course of my consulting career, I've worked with leaders who have had to handle tremendous amounts of adversity. I have seen people respond in different ways. For some leaders, the response is to dig deeper and push through the turbulent times. One example is a client I worked with in the energy industry. Her organization was thrown off guard by a hostile takeover. As the head of HR, she had to support her people while trying to work with the CEO and C-suite to figure out what was going to happen to their company. It was a period of fear, anxiety, and paranoia for many of her employees. She could have easily given up under the pressure and succumbed to the fear her people were experiencing. Instead, she served as a lighthouse for colleagues during the storm. She reinforced the commitment the company had to their people and their desire to prevent the hostile takeover. It took almost a year to work through the adversity, but she was able to keep her people focused on their priorities.

I've also coached leaders who have struggled with adversity. The stress and anxiety that occur when things go wrong can be too much for some people. They tend to lose their focus and at times make things worse than they really are. One example of this was a client I worked with in retail. His team was going through a rough sales cycle, and he fell into the trap of worrying about where business would come from. Instead of motivating and inspiring people to push through the tough times, he began cutting jobs. He reduced the amount of time and resources that were committed to employee engagement and leadership development and began leading with an iron fist. This caused more stress and anxiety on his people and created a negative downward spiral. His business struggled for a long time, and he ultimately was not able to pull his team out of the situation. He eventually was asked to step down from his leadership role, and another team member was asked to take the reins. Had he invested in serving as a motivating and galvanizing force for his people, the situation may have turned out differently.

It is important to remember that any commitment worth keeping is worth giving your all. When trials and tribulations occur, and they always will, it is important to embrace the moment and push through. Some of the best leadership development experiences are figuring out how to get through the tough times. It becomes a growth opportunity for leaders and their teams. The key is not to get frustrated and give up. You have to maintain your effort and momentum. This is not only important for your own growth, but it has an impact on the people around you. When team members see their leaders staying focused and committed, they tend to do the same. How you handle adversity sets an example for the people around you. Make sure you are setting the right example by remaining steadfast in your beliefs and not compromising your leadership to get through the difficult periods.

Never use excuses

Commitment is not about excuses. It is about remaining focused on accomplishing your objectives despite challenges or negative circumstances. Leaders who practice this behavior have the ability to persevere. However, when leaders use excuses and look to blame everything and everyone for their troubles, they tend to derail quickly. I once worked with a consumer-products executive who had this very problem. She was the head of training for her organization and believed her processes and procedures were the best way to develop people. She was not open to input or feedback from her internal customers. This caused a lot of friction and conflict when people wanted to work with her and her team. I was asked to work with her in a coaching capacity to help prevent her from derailing her career with the company. From the first day we met, she was negative and defensive. She did not believe a 360-degree assessment was needed. It was all her internal customers that had the problems and issues. She came up with excuse after excuse as to why they were wrong, and she was right. She begrudgingly agreed to doing the 360-degree assessment. I spoke with close to fifteen of her colleagues and internal customers. The resounding feedback was that she was not open to their ideas, believed her approach was best, and would shut people out if they disagreed with her.

When I met her to share the 360 feedback, she almost kicked me out of her office! She fervently argued with each and every point of feedback that I raised. She had multiple reasons as to why she was not the one causing the issues. I was fighting a lost cause. She was never going to accept responsibility for her actions. Unfortunately, this engagement did not have a happy ending. She continued to come up with excuses and blame others for the recurring conflicts that took place. Several months after we completed our engagement, she was asked to leave the company.

When it comes to achieving your goals and dreams, remember to always accept full responsibility for your actions. You cannot be committed to a desired outcome and quickly look to blame other people or circumstances when things do not go your way. Those who commit to something must have the fortitude to work through the good and bad times. In the end, using excuses only slows things down and makes it extremely hard to remain committed to your key objectives. Commitment is not for the faint of heart. You have to be willing to put in the time and effort needed if you want to achieve your end result. Keep this in mind as you chart a course with your people, and make sure to always keep your eye on the prize. This will drive commitment in your personal efforts and set the right tone for others to follow.

VIGILANCE

Success is a journey, not a destination. It requires
constant effort, vigilance, and reevaluation.

—Mark Twain

Kevin was a new CEO for a shipping and logistics company. He came to the organization to turn things around. The company had spent years in stagnation and working with inefficient processes and procedures. The culture was slow and laid-back, and leaders did not hold one another accountable. His mandate was simple: reengineer the company's operating policies and procedures and reenergize the workforce by instilling vigilant discipline and accountability at all levels of the organization.

Kevin came to my firm with several requests. The first was to help him develop a new leadership competency framework. This would be modeled by his senior leadership team with their people across the company. He also wanted his team to understand the new leadership mandate and begin to drive accountability for results. This was a challenge given that many of his direct reports were part of the old guard. He needed to replace several leaders who were not willing to adjust to his disciplined approach.

Once the leadership framework was in place, we began development assessments with each of his team members. The goal was to identify their strengths and development opportunities against the leadership framework and craft development plans for each leader. As expected, driving disciplined execution came up as a challenge across his senior leadership team. This did not discourage Kevin. He met with each functional leader and made sure they were clear on goals and expectations and began conducting regular follow-up meetings to ensure progress was being made against stated expectations.

As time progressed, the organization went through positive and negative periods. Over the course of one fiscal year, we saw the team go through an acquisition, replace their head of sales, and bring in a new marketing leader. This all was taking place as they were integrating a new IT ERP system. Talk about drastic change! Throughout all of this transition, Kevin remained steadfast and determined to make sure results were being delivered. He continued his regular monthly follow-up meetings with his direct reports. He instructed them to begin instilling monthly one-on-one meetings with their people. Additionally, he started to implement monthly team status meetings. This served as an opportunity for cross-functional colleagues to share information across their many enterprise-wide initiatives.

Kevin pushed his team to be responsible and take ownership for decisions. He vetted ideas from people, defined success metric up front, scoped and resourced projects, defined clear accountabilities, and tracked real progress. It was his ability to use structure, process, and clear expectations that kept people focused on the right outcomes. Over the course of our work with Kevin and his team, we saw a dramatic turnaround in the company's focus and execution. It took a while; but with careful attention to detail and prioritizing effectively, the best use of talent, time, and resources was allocated to driving major business priorities.

Kevin instilled a sense of urgency in his team and organization. This helped to shape the culture and made leaders proactive in their approach to problems. They took decisive actions instead of waiting for others to get the job done. Today, his organization operates with a strong results-oriented culture. People challenge one another to improve day-to-day processes in order to drive current and future outcomes. The company is consistent in exceeding shareholder goals and expectations because of the discipline and rigor Kevin instilled with his people. He was able to raise the bar on performance by leading with vigilance.

The Critical Components of Vigilant Leadership

Vigilance is about discipline, execution, and accountability. People who exercise these three skills are effective in moving things forward. They are focused on what needs to be accomplished and hold both themselves and others accountable to delivering results. At the core of discipline is the ability to set and follow healthy and productive habits. In his book *The Power of Habit*, Charles Duhigg explores research on the science of habits and, in particular, how habits impact people at an individual and organizational level. He outlines that there is no quick fix or winning formula for starting, stopping, and changing habits. However, Duhigg does provide a clear and concise framework for understanding how habits work and a powerful guide to experimenting how they can be changed. His framework includes four critical components. First, a person must identify their routines, which consist of a cue, a routine, and a reward. These three components serve as a continuous loop that strengthen and reinforce habits.

From a leadership standpoint, the habit loop can be used to identify how strengths manifest themselves and how development gaps prevent leaders from productive work outcomes. When a leader wants to start a new habit, they can identify specific cues that will help to initiate a routine behavior, which will lead to a specific reward or desired outcome. For example, take the average sales leader. One habit loop routine might involve making calls to prospective clients to sell new products or services. The cue could be walking up to their desk at the office and sitting in the chair. This could trigger a routine that would involve calling several potential clients for new sales opportunities. The reward would be generating new client sales. Over time, if this routine is practiced regularly, a habit will form where as soon as the sales leader sees their desk and chair, it will trigger the need to begin making sales calls to generate new business.

The habit loop can also be used to change behaviors by supplementing old vices with new routines. For example, let's say that a leader easily gets frustrated with people during his team meetings and ends up needing to take a break to go outside for a cigarette. The leader would first have to identify the components of their loop (e.g., a direct report repeats themselves or says something incorrect, which leads to unnecessary conversation, which leads to frustration and anger, which leads to the need for a cigarette break) and then begin to work on changing one or more of the elements in the routine.

This leads to the second factor in Duhigg's model, experimenting with rewards. In our example, the leader could start to experiment with different outcomes rather than stepping out to have a cigarette. One day, he could take a walk down to the cafeteria to buy a candy bar, another day he could walk back to his office to get a piece of gum, and the third day he could walk to the vending machine and purchase a protein bar. The key is to identify what feelings and emotions are felt after the reward so that a new reward can replace the need for a cigarette. By experimenting with different rewards, leaders can isolate specific behaviors in order to redesign habit patterns.

The third component involves isolating specific cues that trigger the start of a habit loop. Sticking with our example from the preceding paragraph, the cue for our leader involves direct reports repeating themselves or sharing incorrect information that take the team down an unnecessary path of conversation. In order to get a better understanding of how the trigger initiates their routine, the leader can identify categories of behaviors ahead of time in order to begin to see patterns. Is it their emotional state during a particular part of the conversation? Is it related to a specific person who usually says incorrect or unnecessary things? Is it related to a particular time during the meeting? Is it typically during a specific topic or agenda item during the meeting? By identifying the specific nature of the cues, the leader can move on to the fourth component, developing a new plan. Once a leader can identify their habit loop—determining what trigger is causing a routine that leads to a specific reward—they can change to a better habit routine by planning for the cue and choosing a behavior that leads to a more productive reward. The key takeaway about habits is that every habit starts with a choice that we deliberately make and then at some point stop thinking about but continue to make every day. Good habits take focus and concerted effort in the beginning, but as we continue to practice the behavior, they become automatic routines.

The Power of Execution

Moving beyond habits and discipline is the importance of execution. Vigilant leaders know how to execute effectively. They establish role clarity and ownership for deliverables, time lines, and key milestones. I've had the opportunity to work with many leaders who do this extremely well. One leader in particular made it his top priority to use structure, process, and clear expectation to keep people focused on the right issues. When we started our coaching work together, he would meet once a month with each of his direct reports to ensure progress was being made against the individual goals. He also had quarterly team meetings to focus on collective outcomes. Many leaders talk a good game when it comes to regular one-on-ones with their team members, but this leader brought it to life. Regardless of his schedule or commitments, he made sure to keep this focus on execution and driving performance.

Leaders who are skilled in getting others to execute also prioritize effectively so that the best use of talent, time, and resources can be allocated to the right issues. They are quick to tackle internal and external obstacles to execution. They drive a sense of urgency into the work so people understand the importance of sticking to the task at hand. When leaders struggle prioritizing time and resources, execution becomes a challenge. I've coached leaders who become easily distracted by new ideas or "flavor of the month" and have their people focusing on too many objectives at the same time. When this happens, people are not disciplined in their efforts and often have difficulty following through.

When leaders inspire others to execute, there is a collective willingness to challenge each other to improve processes for greater long-term impact. People become focused on what they need to accomplish on a daily basis. They set and consistently exceed goals and expectations, which raises the bar on overall performance. When I have seen leaders do this, they motivate their people to go above and beyond in their work efforts. For example, about several years ago, I coached a pharmaceuticals executive who was always pushing his team to accomplish the next desired outcome. He was not afraid to recruit and select the best people (those who had strengths and competencies outside of his expertise) and challenge each team member to strive for their very best on a consistent basis. This created a healthy sense of competition on the team and enabled people to exceed expectations. It also created a culture within his function that operated with a very strong results orientation. Even though he was relentless in driving people to execute on their priorities, he took time to celebrate the victories along the way. This showed people that he valued their efforts and recognized high quality work.

Holding People Accountable

The final component of vigilant leadership is accountability. Strong leaders know how to hold people accountable for results. They take personal ownership for taking vision and translating it into practical actions that others can follow. Accountability requires clearly defined priorities and expectations, discipline, and follow-through. People have to be committed to one another as well as their leader for accountability to work. Leaders need to balance a sense of urgency with an understanding of the breaking point of people on their team. They must also be willing to make tough decisions when employees do not follow through on their commitments. Accountability can only work if there are rewards for achievement and consequences for failing to meet expectations.

I've had the opportunity to work with leaders who are great at holding people accountable. One leader I worked with was in sales for a large financial services company. She was not afraid to make the tough call if people were not meeting expectations. During our yearlong coaching engagement, I witnessed her remove several people from their roles due to failure in following through on delivering results. She communicated to all her team members that people would be held accountable to certain performance targets and that there would be consequences if they did not hit their targets. When she kept her word and held people accountable, it did not create fear but reinforced the effort and commitment of her team. It also made them set realistic and practical goals—ones they felt were a challenge but believed they could attain.

I've also coached leaders who have difficulty holding team members accountable. When I work with these types of leaders, they typically have challenges keeping their word or have issues with following through. I remember working with a leader from a small manufacturing company. He was notorious for giving people assignments and responsibilities and then never making sure people reached the desired outcome. Part of this was that he was easily distracted. There was always another exciting project he wanted to undertake, so there became an issue of having too many things going on at the same time. He was also was a big people pleaser, so it was hard to have the tough conversations when people needed to be held accountable. My coaching work with him evolved around developing greater gravitas and courage. We had to focus on instilling the right behaviors that would allow him to focus on key priorities and not be afraid to make sure people felt responsible for delivering results. It took some time and concerted effort, but he was able to begin narrowing down his interests and making sure people met their performance targets.

Action Steps for Leading with Vigilance

Set specific goals

Vigilant leaders understand the power of S.M.A.R.T. goals, a term coined by George T. Doran in a 1981 issue of *Management Review*. The acronym S.M.A.R.T. stands for *specific, measurable, attainable, relevant*, and *time bound*. For years, leadership and management consultants have leveraged this model in training, coaching, and leadership development. Leaders who set S.M.A.R.T. goals are more likely to achieve their desired outcomes and live successful and fulfilled lives.

Goals that are specific target a particular area of importance. They are clear and concise and outline what's expected. For example, saying that you want to improve sales performance is not a specific goal. However, saying that you want to improve sales performance by 10 percent over the next six months by introducing two new products to the market is very specific. When I partner with my clients to help them build specific goals into their coaching development plans, we tend to see the greatest impact after the engagement has been completed. This usually occurs because specific goals answer the five W questions: What does my client want to accomplish? Why do they want to accomplish this goal (i.e., what's the purpose or benefits to achieving the goal)? Who will need to be involved to help make the goal a reality? Where will the work take place? What requirements, barriers, and constraints could get in the way of goal attainment? Whenever you are setting a goal, use these five questions and you will be well on your way to setting specific goals.

Measurable goals quantify objectives and serve as an indicator of progress for goals. If a leader cannot measure their goal, it becomes impossible for them to know if they are making progress. Using our example from the preceding paragraph, there are two measurable indicators. The first is the 10 percent sales growth. Whether we are at 5 percent or 8 percent, we can track progress against a concrete objective. The second is the six-month time frame. As we move closer to the deadline, we should be closer to the 10 percent target. My clients find this component of the S.M.A.R.T. system the best indicator for helping their teams and organizations track progress over time. People get excited about hitting the measurable objectives and usually become thrilled and excited as they get close to the end of the target objective. This also helps teams exert the continued effort required to reach the final outcome. A measurable goal will answer these three questions: How much time it will take to reach the goal? How many parts will be involved in the goal? How will I know when the goal is accomplished?

Achievable goals are realistic and attainable. They stretch people to go above and beyond their current boundaries but do not push people to the extreme. Goals that are too lofty or too easy do not drive performance. When leaders develop goals that are important and achievable, they can work with others to make the goals a reality. I typically see the most obstacles in goal setting around this area of the S.M.A.R.T. model. Many of my clients will sit down with me and set extremely high goals, objectives that no individual or team can accomplish. For example, I once worked with a R&D executive who wanted his team to develop seven new products by the end of the calendar year. It was July, and the company had not developed any new products in the last three years. To set a goal that high was not attainable. Something more realistic would be to develop one or two new products by year end. This would motivate and galvanize his team, not demoralize them. Achievable goals answer two questions: How can the goal be accomplished? How realistic is the goal based on other circumstances, challenges, or obstacles?

Relevant goals matter. They have personal meaning to the leader and to the team. These types of goals excite people. Goals that are relevant to the leader, their team, and the broader organization receive the most support. When everyone has buy in to the goal, people begin to serve as champions for its attainment. They will work together to knock down obstacles and overcome barriers. They will look for opportunities to contribute and play their part in achieving the objective. I often advise my CEO clients about the importance of setting relevant goals. Their goals need to push the organization forward. They need to resonate with people across cross-functional boundaries. It is great when an overarching goal is supported by smaller objectives that are in alignment with the primary desired outcome. When my clients set relevant goals that connect with their people, they get the best out of others. Here are several questions I ask my clients when setting relevant goals: Is the goal worth achieving? Is it the right time to set this goal? Does the goal align with other efforts within the organization? Is the goal applicable to the company's current strategic priorities?

Time-bound goals specify when the results will be achieved. Here, the importance of grounding goals within a given time frame helps to give a team or organization focus. The commitment to a deadline strengthens people's efforts toward the completion of a goal. In my coaching with senior executives, this component of the S.M.A.R.T. model is used to prevent their goals from being derailed by daily crises. It is inevitable that the challenges of the day will interfere with longer-term goals and objectives. By putting a time-frame around a goal, it keeps people focused on moving toward their desired outcome. It also brings a sense of urgency to their work efforts. When setting time-bound goals, I will ask my clients the following questions: When do they want to achieve their goal by? What do they hope to achieve several months from now? What do they hope to achieve several weeks from now? What is one action can they do today to begin moving toward their goal?

Create strong habits

We spent time earlier in this chapter talking about habits and their importance. I want to reiterate how crucial habit-forming is for any leader. As you map out your personal life and professional career, it is critical to build strong, healthy habits into the framework. I like to think of habit forming on five levels. First, leaders need to address their mental and spiritual needs. Regardless of your religious ideology, every leader should build habits such as prayer, meditation, and reflection into their lives. This helps strengthen resolve and enables people to push through challenging and difficult times. I personally like to start my day in prayer and meditation. It allows me to stay fresh and sets the tone for how I will approach my daily activities. Others like to end their day in prayer or meditation. It helps them to wind down and enables them to get a good night's sleep. Whatever works for you, make sure to build habits that cater to your mental and spiritual needs.

The second level of positive habit-forming is centered around our physical needs. This includes fitness and diet. Leaders who incorporate daily exercise and the proper nutrition program operate at their best. They have more energy to tackle the challenges of the day and bring greater thought and creativity to their work. I encourage my clients to build exercise habits early in their day. Trying to hit the gym or go for a run after a long day can be challenging. Building this habit into your routine on a consistent basis will give you a lifetime of energy and vitality.

Next come relational habits. We all need encouragement and support from our loved ones. We can also offer our families and friends the support they need to tackle their days. Look for opportunities to spend quality time with those closest to you. It can be breakfast in the morning, taking time for a nice lunch break, or dinner with the family in the evenings. Making sure to spend time with those we care about most helps create a healthy work-life balance. Good relational habits also impact us at work. Mentoring and coaching, whether this is with direct reports or with cross-functional colleagues, helps strengthen people. I regularly encourage my clients to make sure they have consistent one-on-ones with their team members not just for status updates on projects but to help people grow. Some of my clients have gone a step further and have developed mentoring programs for their organizations. This is a great way to strengthen relationships and help develop people for the future.

Career habits help shape our professional destiny. This category of habit setting is not just about getting the next promotion. It is about taking time to identify our hopes and dreams over the course of one's career. Do you want to start your own company one day? Do you have dreams of becoming a CEO? Do you have a passion for creating products? Do you want to impact people on the largest stage? The first step is taking time to map out the next five, ten, and fifteen years. You can start by outlining goals that you want to attain and then putting in place some habits to make those objectives a reality. For example, if you want to start your own business one day, some habits you could put in place include (a) identifying and reading books about starting your own business, (b) seeking out people who have built their own business and learning from them, (c) attending conferences or workshops on building a business, (d) developing a business plan or strategy for how you will launch your company, and (e) identify and meet with potential investors. Leaders who set good career habits achieve their professional desires. They put in place consistent behaviors to help move them in the right direction for the future.

Lastly, we should all spend time on civic habits. This is about creating rhythms of volunteering and charitable work. Some leaders do this by volunteering with nonprofit organizations or through their religious places of worship. Others give back to the community through charitable donations or spending time to help people in need. Whatever your interests are, find some way to give back to others. This gives perspective and helps create a fully balanced life-style. It also allows you to practice the behavior of giving back. Many of us have been blessed with great jobs and careers. Giving back to those who are less fortunate makes us even more thankful for what we have.

Get an accountability partner

As I mentioned earlier, vigilance is hard work! It takes a special person to cultivate disciplined effort day in and day out. Finding an accountability partner makes this much easier. Your accountability partner should keep you honest and focused toward putting in consistent work that is required to get you to your desired outcome. Pick someone who cares about you and your goals/objectives but isn't afraid to give you that tough love when it is needed. We all need that extra push from time to time, so find an accountability partner who will help you exercise greater levels of vigilance as time progresses.

Several years ago, one of my clients put this behavior into practice across all areas of her life. At work, she had her company invest in executive coaching. As her coach, I met with her once a month for close to a year. At the start of our engagement, we set a number of S.M.A.R.T. goals, and then during each of our coaching sessions, I followed up to make sure she was taking action in each area. This kept her accountable to making progress. She also partnered with several cross-functional colleagues on some larger organizational initiatives. The peer-to-peer accountability helped all the team members remain focused on their key objectives. In her personal life, she got an accountability partner for working out and going to the gym. Her personal trainer kept her honest and disciplined with her daily workout regimen. He also motivated her to keep her diet and workout schedule as a top priority. At home, she asked her husband to work with her on keeping family commitments (e.g., having a family dinner a few nights a week, time with their children, date night, etc.) and not letting work become all consuming.

Accountability partners keep us vigilant. They are people who care about our growth and development but will push us to get to that next level. Look for accountability partners whom you trust and those who know you well. They should have a thorough understanding of where your strengths and development opportunities are so that they can help you maximize your impact. The best accountability partners will be there for you through thick and thin. They are great sources for feedback and input along the way.

Prioritize and work your plan

Prioritization is everything. As Stephen R. Covey put it, "Put first things first." That means it is critical to prioritize the daily activities that are most important to us. For example, if your goal is to lose twenty pounds, starting your day with a workout might be important. Putting it off until the end of the day when you might be tired or drained will impact your long-term ability to stick with the gym. As you prioritize your most important activities, it is also important to stick to the plan you outlined. This means using your accountability partner to work the plan. It also means being flexible enough to make changes along the way that will help you achieve your goal.

I often advise my clients to prioritize their most important goals and objectives. At the start of our consulting or coaching engagement, we will sit down and build out their personal development plan. We outline the top three to four objectives that they wish to accomplish and then begin prioritizing what is most important for them. For example, I recently worked with a CFO from a small biotech pharmaceutical company. He had several key objectives that were critical to reorganizing the finance function. First, we determined that he had to reduce the company's expense allocations. If this wasn't addressed, the company would continue to lose money on unnecessary spending. Then we had to focus on building out the finance leadership team. He needed a good controller as well as several VPs. Lastly, he had to build a strong partnership with the CEO and his peers on the executive leadership team. By prioritizing what was most important, we were able to address the most critical issues and work the plan.

Working the plan is just as important as prioritization. Leaders can do this by practicing some of the behaviors I outlined above (e.g., setting good habits, and working with an accountability partner), but they can also enlist the help of others to accomplish their objectives. In the preceding example with the biotech CFO, once he put in place a strong finance leadership team, he began giving each of his direct reports several important responsibilities that aligned with his top priorities. This enabled him to distribute the duties and responsibilities and get things completed in a timely and efficient manner.

Remember, vigilance takes time, focus, and effort. Practicing the behaviors outlined in this chapter will help you achieve your goals and become a better leader. It will also help you to set a positive example for the people around you. People are drawn to strong role models. Vigilant leaders can set the tone for others to follow and instill the proper sense of urgency to drive key objectives. Moving on from vigilance, our next leadership competency focuses on consistency. This leadership skill goes hand-in-hand with vigilance as the two set the foundation for the influence we have on others.

CONSISTENCY

It's not what we do once in a while. that shapes
our destiny. It's what we do consistently.

—Tony Robbins

Christina was the CEO for a specialty clothing retailer. She was
a veteran of the industry with over thirty years of experience. She
was recruited into the organization to drive sales and revenue growth
over a five-year period. In the first several years, the company had
tremendous growth. They adjusted their strategic plan to go after a
larger market that focused on customers in the thirteen-to-twenty-
two age range. This enabled the company to offer several different
product categories (e.g., boys and girls clothing, jewelry, accessories,
and perfumes) for their customers. They built out an e-commerce
platform and put in place an omnichannel marketing strategy. They
updated their IT infrastructure and put in place an ERP software
system. They began identifying and selecting A-player talent for key
roles throughout the leadership team and organization. Things were
really starting to fall into place for Christina and her organization
until major adversity hit the business.

At a macrolevel, the teenage and adolescent specialty clothing
retail industry hit a major slump. Competitors were cutting costs
left and right to survive. Christina had to do the same with her
organization. Month after month, they missed their revenue targets. SG&A expenses started to become a serious problem for the
company. Christina and her executive leadership team had to keep
SG&A expenses under tight control and limited to a certain percent-
age of revenue by reducing corporate overhead (i.e., cost-cutting and
employee layoffs). This affected the company in a major way. People

began fearing for their jobs and performance suffered greatly. Despite all these challenges, Christina remained steadfast in her approach to managing the business. She led with personal courage and high integrity at all times. She presented a calm and composed demeanor around her direct reports and in monthly town halls to the entire organization. As bad news continued to pour in from the market, she continued to communicate the challenges and difficult news to various stakeholders in a straightforward and honest manner. Christina demonstrated the courage of her convictions by showing up every day at 7:00 a.m. and staying until 8:00 p.m. to work through critical issues with her team. I began coaching her around this time to help her navigate through all the challenges that she faced from a leadership and talent perspective.

When we first sat down to outline an agenda and plan of attack, she shared her fears and doubts about the future viability of the company. She had to revisit her executive leadership team's structure and make some tough decisions with regards to letting go of key leaders a level below the senior team. Although it was an extremely difficult time for Christina, I was impressed with her ability to understand and embrace the burden of leadership. She made the tough decisions with respect to letting people go but dealt with these issues in a pragmatic, emotionally mature, and even-handed manner.

After close to eighteen months of economic challenges and declining revenues, things slowly began to improve. Foot traffic in their stores across the country began to pick up. Customers were buying again. Throughout this transition period, Christina solicited the input and counsel from her direct reports to strengthen the business in each of their respective areas of expertise. She also continued to work with my firm to rebuild their culture and focus on talent development. We conducted a culture survey to examine the current levels of employee engagement. The feedback was tough to swallow, but once again, Christina took the information to heart. She took action to regain people's confidence in the company's vision, their mission, and their hopes for the future. She was authentic in her leadership and showed people she was motivated by more than personal gain. She made every effort to refocus people on the core attributes of the organization's culture while proactively seeking to enhance it. Employees began to respond positively to her efforts. The business and employee morale continued to improve for the organization. She was hopeful and reenergized for the future until a devastating personal tragedy struck her family.

Christina had three children: two sons, ages nineteen and twenty-two, and one daughter, who was twenty-six. Her youngest son had recently started college and was attending a large state university. One night, her son was out drinking with friends, and one of the young men decided to drive the group across town for a party. They got to the party and continued to drink and socialize. On their ride back, the driver fell asleep at the wheel, and the car hit a tree on the side of the road. Christina's son was thrown from the vehicle and passed away before the ambulance could arrive. Christina and her husband received the call at 2:00 a.m. Their world came crashing down upon hearing the news.

I was scheduled to meet with Christina three days after the tragic event took place. Despite the funeral preparations and other family-related issues, she still wanted to meet. She spent most of our session crying and confused. How could this have happened to her son? How was their family going to be able to move forward? How were they going to be able to pick up all the pieces? I offered all the support and encouragement that I could, but it was an extremely painful and difficult time for Christina and her family.

Her direct reports and the broader organization were all supportive. Her COO told Christina to take some time off to be with her husband and children. Although she was hurting tremendously, Christina continued to show up to work day after day. She was one of the first cars in the parking lot and was one of the last people to leave the building. This steadfast personal courage despite all the negative things that her family was going through was truly inspirational to others. Make no mistake, Christina and her family were going through an extremely dark period. There were days when she would just call me to talk about how her husband was doing or how much she missed her son. However, her focus and determination with the business did not waver. When tragedies like this occur, some leaders will hunker down and focus more on their business. It helps them to compartmentalize and get through the difficult periods. I saw this in action with Christina. She continued to have her moments of difficulty during her grieving period, but her resolve grew stronger over time.

Christina embodied the competency of consistency. During difficult times in the business, she remained calm under pressure and delivered on her commitments. She demonstrated the courage of her convictions and set an example for others to follow. She inspired trust through her daily behaviors and always operated in an open, honest, and transparent manner. When personal tragedy struck her family, she continued to do what was necessary for the business and acted with unquestionable ethics and integrity. Her personal morale compass served as a beacon of hope and encouragement to her employees. She is a great example of being a true ambassador of consistency in both words and actions.

Consistency Matters

Consistency is about character, courage, and integrity. It's about walking the talk. I've seen it demonstrated in the best fashion with many professional athletes. Michael Jordan, Peyton Manning, Derek Jeter, Kobe Bryant, Lebron James, and Tom Brady are just a few of the examples of athletic leaders who demonstrate consistency day in and day out. They walk the talk. They understand that setting a positive example for others speaks louder than words.

I've had the pleasure of getting to know some sports psychologists who had personally worked with Kobe Bryant. We all saw the game-winning shots, the five championships, the numerous all-star appearances. What we did not see is the work he put in to accomplish those great feats. Kobe was consistently the first one in the gym at 5:00 a.m. He would work on his shot over and over again, sometimes shooting until he would hit fifty to sixty shots in a row. He did this from all over the court. Next, he would work on his dribbling and ball-handling skills. After that, he would be in the weight room for two hours. This was all before any of his teammates would even show up at the practice facility! He led by example in practice, pushed his teammates during games, and constantly strived to make everyone better. He was a tireless competitor. For Kobe, it was all about winning. His consistency did not stop with basketball practice, though. It carried over into how he took care of his physical body, by the food that he ate, and by the amount of time he took for rest and sleep. He did this over and over again throughout his illustrious career. No wonder he will go down as one of the greatest in the sport of professional basketball!

The Three Components of Consistency

Character

Our background and upbringing matter. This is where we develop character traits that will impact us for the rest of our lives. Some of the most effective leaders whom I have worked with have stories from their past that help shape who they are today. This typically begins in early childhood. It's the simple things that parents should teach their children—manners at the dinner table, asking for things politely, saying please and thank you. These early life lessons begin to shape our character. It shapes how we will interact with the world later in life.

This is not the only place where character traits are born. Many of our character traits are formed by modeling the behaviors of others at a very young age. This starts with parents but extends to the broader family circle, to friends and acquaintances during formative school years, and to coaches, teachers, and role models later in high school. I've seen this time and time again with many of the executives I work with. Most of them can recall a person or experience from their childhood that left a strong impression on them. I hear stories like, "My father's work ethic helped shape how I approach my work today," "My dance instructor taught me the importance of focus and never giving up," "My mother showed people respect and compassion. I learned to do the same with others," "My high school coach taught me what it meant to have discipline and commitment," "My grandfather taught me to look for the best in people."

Just as these positive experiences helped to shape the lives of some executives, I've also heard of negative experiences serving as character building moments. I have had clients talk about seeing a parent dealing with addiction, about two parents going through a divorce, about the death of a family member or friend, or about the environment where they grew up. I once worked with a retail executive who had a fascinating background and story. Tim grew up in the poverty-ridden streets of the Chicago projects. His father left before he was born. His mother was in and out of rehab facilities numerous times. Tim and his two older brothers were raised primarily by their grandmother. He saw his oldest brother get pulled into gangs and the drug game. This all took place before he was seventeen years old! Now given his environment and upbringing, one could argue that he would follow in the steps of his oldest brother. However, all the negativity around Tim made him look at the world through a very different lens. He wanted to get himself out of the projects. He wanted to have a better life for himself and his future. So at eighteen, Tim joined the marines. He quickly rose to the top of his call, and worked on his education after his two tours in Iraq. He successfully transitioned into the professional sector after serving his time in the military. He told me that it was those early life experiences that helped shape his character.

As leaders, our character sets the stage for how we will interact with others, how we will treat people, and how we will impact performance. Leaders who have used their upbringing and early life experiences to shape strong characters—those marked by honesty, fairness, and respect for people—have the greatest influence. This is because character determines how we will navigate both the good and bad times. A leader who is honest will report sales performance when they hit their targets and when they struggle to do so. A fair leader will reward pay for performance. They won't show favoritism. A leader who respects people will treat colleagues from different ethnic and racial backgrounds the same. Our character serves as a foundation setting component to our leadership effectiveness.

Courage

Consistency is about having the courage of your convictions. It's about standing up for something you believe in and seeing it through until the end. Courage is developed with practice. It does not happen overnight. Life circumstances dictate how well we develop this skill. We have all heard the saying "Life is 10 percent what happens to you, and the other 90 percent is how you handle it." Courage falls in the 90 percent range. I've seen leaders develop courage in some of the most difficult and trying conditions. I've also seen clients struggle with demonstrating courage and the results have been catastrophes.

One of my clients in the medical devices sector demonstrated courage under fire. His business had enjoyed three consecutive years of increased revenues and profits. During this time, he focused on growing his leadership team, strengthening the capabilities of his direct reports, and putting in place a strong high-potential leadership development program. Going into year four, the economic landscape started to shift. At the end of their first quarter, he saw sales drop by 20 percent. The overall trend for the year did not look promising. Given this news, my client had two choices staring him in the face. On the one hand, he could cut SG&A and focus on driving revenue with an intense execution. On the other hand, he could continue to work on developing his team and reinforce their focus on sales execution. The easy thing to do would be to drop all the work that was invested into his team and the broader organization. Expenses needed to be cut, and this is typically the first thing that gets cut. However, my client took a firm stance on his belief that leadership development made his people better. It helped them to drive customer service and sales force excellence in the field. He chose to keep the programs going that helped to prepare people for the future. We stuck with the high-potential program. We kept the team effectiveness work with his leadership team. They missed revenue targets two quarters that year but saw the back half of the year have a strong surge. To this day, my client looks at that period as a moment that tested his courage and commitment to his people. He had the courage to stick to what he believed was the right thing to do, even though contextual and situational factors told him to take a different course.

I've also seen courage displayed at the direct report versus manager level. I recently worked with an HR director who worked for a leader who liked to cut corners. This leader treated people unfairly and engaged in risky behaviors (e.g., excessive drinking and partying with direct reports). The HR director knew that the leader was going to get the entire team into trouble by some of these behaviors. She saw the writing on the wall. However, she was put in a tough predicament. Should she confront her manager and tell him the behavior was inappropriate? Should she go to her dotted-line manager, the VP of HR, and tell him what was going on? Should she say nothing and hope things would change for the better? We spoke about her options at length. It was a difficult conversation. She feared that she would be fired if she confronted her manager, and he took things the wrong way. However, she knew what the right thing was and what needed to be done. She stood behind the courage of her convictions and confronted her manager about his inappropriate behaviors. The conversation did not go well. She could have dropped things there, but no, she stuck to her guns and got her dotted-line manager involved. Within four weeks, an HR investigation was launched, and her manager was fired for several inappropriate behaviors that were against company policy and procedures. Through this experience, my client strengthened her muscles of courage.

There is a powerful relationship between courage and character. A strong background and upbringing helps to solidify behaviors that lead to character development. Once a leader's character takes shape, the choices and decisions they regularly exercise typically involve courage. It takes courage to do the right things when the wrong things are easier to do. It takes courage to stand behind one's values and beliefs and be willing to challenge colleagues when they are not doing the same. It takes courage to lead through difficult times when the people around you want to give up and quit. When a leader is consistent in demonstrating courage, they begin to serve as a positive role model for others. People want to do the right things because they see their leader setting the right example.

Integrity

Leadership is reflected by attitude. Attitude is shaped by integrity. Leaders with high integrity understand and embrace the burdens as well as the benefits of leadership. They live by strong values and guiding principles that shape how they interact with others and manage their business. Like character, people develop integrity based on early life experiences. They are taught—by parents, family, friends, or other early life role models—how to respect people, how to treat others, and how to carry themselves in the public arena. Some of the most effective leaders I've worked with operate from a foundation of high integrity. They tend to be motivated by more than personal gain or achievement. They promote the greater good of the organization. They inspire trust through both words and actions. They communicate good and bad news to colleagues in a straightforward and honest manner.

When integrity is missing, problems quickly arise. I can remember this happening for a client I worked with in the energy industry. He approached most of his interactions with a win-lose mind-set. He was highly competitive with people and always had to come out ahead. This would often cause him to treat people as means to an end rather than as colleagues. Early in his career, this was not much of a problem as he was an individual contributor and could focus more on his duties and responsibilities. However, once he got into management, things started to fall apart. His tendency to treat people disrespectfully and always having to get his way caused a lot of friction with his direct reports and with cross-functional peers.

When I started coaching him, there were some pretty significant gaps in his leadership. However, before we could get into any of his behaviors, we needed to identify what mattered most to him. His core values and beliefs. I needed to know where the self-interest originated from. Did he come from a family with a lot of brothers and sisters where competition was valued? Did he go through some early life experiences that made him develop such a strong sense of self-entitlement? What were his core values? Did he value power? Security? Influence? We had to uncover his guiding principles in order to have a framework through which we could drive behavior change.

After our first few coaching meetings, it became clear where his values and beliefs came from. As an adolescent, he was a top athlete in track and field. He was a 200m and 400m runner. Everything involved in his training was based on competing with others. He looked at other track athletes as foes he had to beat. He was also one of three boys growing up. Both of his brothers were older than him. He always put pressure on himself to do better than his older siblings. He brought this mind-set into relationships in high school and college. It quickly became clear that throughout his life he was rewarded for winning. His belief system was formed around striving to be his best and outperforming those around him. Once we identified his core belief system, we began to work on changing some of his guiding principles. He no longer had to lead with a winner takes all mentality. We started shifting the attention to team effectiveness. He began to see that "to win" meant his team being successful. It meant that he had to start taking time to build solid relationships with others. He had to start thinking about the thoughts and feelings of colleagues and lead with greater integrity.

Leading with integrity is about servant leadership. That is, putting others before your personal interests and demonstrating the same actions and behaviors daily. It's about modeling the things you want your people to do. I've seen many clients who do this, and the results they achieve are very impressive. When they set a vision, hold people accountable to results, and then model the way the team should perform, the sky is the limit to overall performance.

Action Steps for Leading with Consistency

Get your guiding principles in order

To lead with consistency, you first need to identify your most important values and beliefs. What are your guiding principles? Do you value affiliation? Influence? Tradition? Recognition? Aesthetics? Find out what really matters to you. I will often start an executive coaching engagement by asking my clients four questions: What's most important to you? What beliefs did you learn growing up? What values do you live by today? Where have you fallen short in staying true to your core principles? These questions get a leader in the right frame of mind to explore their personal belief system. Once we have identified what matters most, we move on to outlining what they want their new values to be. Perhaps they oversee a large team and they want the team to value honesty, accountability, and a passion for the business. They might be a subject matter expert and want their core beliefs to be commitment, achievement, and perseverance. As a leader, you need to get clarity on what you want your values to be.

Once you've identified your personal values and belief system, it is important to build out the core principles of your team or organization. This can be done in various ways. I advise my clients to take their teams through a values and beliefs exercise that gets the team to begin thinking about their collective guiding principles. The team-building exercise is called Moments that Matter, and it involves team members sharing personal life experiences that helped shape their core belief systems. When I do this exercise, I have team members sit in a large circle around a room. We instruct people to go around the room and share one success story and one lesson learned that helped shape their values. As we move around the room, one person keeps tabs of the values and beliefs that are shared by everyone. At the end of the exercise, my clients typically have a list of guiding principles that they can revise, modify, and ratify as the team's collective core values. This is a powerful exercise as it lets every team member contribute to the creation of a team value system.

At the organizational level, it is important to have shared core values across functions and business units. Developing enterprise core values typically begins with the formation of a leadership competency model that can be used to develop an organization's core values system. One of my financial services clients did this for their organization. They started the process by developing a leadership competency model for their most senior executives. This model guided how they were to behave and lead each of their respective functions and business units. From this senior leadership model, we helped our client cascade the leadership framework to lower levels of the organization. At the end of the process, there was a leadership competency framework for every level, from c-suite executives down to entry-level managers. These leadership frameworks were then used to develop a shared core values system for employees across the organization. In the end, the company had a shared core values system that was directly linked to leadership effectiveness.

You have to get your guiding principles in order if you're going to lead with consistency. Consistent leaders operate from a strong base of core beliefs. These values do not change over time. They serve as the true north under good and bad circumstances. They help shape the actions and behaviors of a team and organization. Remember to get clear on what's most important to you; your values will guide your decision making every day.

Outline your ethical code of conduct

Guiding principles are the starting point for leading with consistency. Consistent leaders also live by an ethical code of conduct. This is the rules of engagement for how leader's team members are to respect each other, their customers, and others in the organization. The ethical code of conduct is different from a guiding principle. The former focuses how leaders will work together. The latter focuses on core beliefs of a team or organization. As an example, a team's core value could be trust, defined as a firm reliance on the integrity, ability, or character of another person. The code of conduct that brings the value of trust to life could be (a) team members are open and transparent with each other, (b) team members are honest in their interactions with customers, and (c) team members respect the background and diversity on the team. So the questions become, What is the way you want your people to behave? How do you want them to interact and partner with one another? What are your nonnegotiables? It's important to outline what you will stand for and make clear what will not be tolerated. Share this with your team and make sure all people are aligned and on the same page.

I recently worked with a senior executive team where we developed and put into practice a code of ethics. The team was just forming with several new leaders to the organization. The leader of the team wanted to get everyone on the same page. So I met with the team leader, and we outlined her guiding principles. Some of these included innovation, efficiency, fairness, and fun. Once we had her guiding principles in order, it was important to solicit input from all the team members. I interviewed each of the twelve team members to learn about their value systems and identify what values the team should live by. Their individual lists were aggregated, and we added several guiding principles for the team. These included diversity, recognition, and structure. We now had seven guiding principles (innovation, efficiency, fairness, fun, diversity, recognition, and structure) for the team.

Next, we scheduled a full day offsite to define the team values and create the ethical code of conduct. At the offsite, it was important to have the team come up with clear definitions for each of the seven guiding principles. This would help them develop the rules of engagement for each value. We spent most of the morning talking through the seven principles and how to best define them. For illustration purposes, we will use diversity as our example. The team defined it as "embracing thoughts and ideas from various backgrounds, culture, and experiences." Once we had the definition, we began outlining the diversity code of conduct. There were three components to the ethical code for diversity: (a) team members will give each other the space to share their ideas; b) team members will respect the background (e.g., gender, race, age, sexual orientation) of one another; and (c) team members will encourage a diversity of thought and input on all major strategic decisions for the team. We developed an ethical code for all seven guiding principles in this manner. By the end of the day, the team had their guiding principles and their ethical code of conduct.

The code of conduct needs to be something that the leader reinforces on a consistent basis. People will quickly ignore the ethical code if there is no accountability to it. I've seen this happen with many teams. They put a great code of conduct on paper. It hangs on walls so everyone can see it, but the leader does not reinforce the right behaviors. This is one of the fastest ways to derail collective performance.

Model the right behaviors

Having guiding principles and an ethical code of conduct is a great way to drive consistency. However, the best leaders consistently model the right behaviors for others. This not only applies to values and conduct; it permeates through all aspects of performance. Is the leader one of the first ones in the office and one of the last to leave? Does the leader model cooperation and teamwork? Do they build sustainable relationships by treating others with respect and dignity? Do they put in the work and effort to accomplish goals? Do they avoid taking shortcuts and quick fixes to deal with problems?

Leaders need to model the appropriate behaviors for others. They inspire others in the greatest way when people believe that they stand for something greater than personal gain. When integrity is one of a leader's highest values, they do not settle for cutting corners or taking shortcuts. They practice what they preach, and it resonates with others. Modeling the right behaviors is so important to effective leadership. You cannot influence others if they do not believe in what you stand for; if your actions are not congruent with the words that you preach.

So how can you model the right behaviors with greater consistency? We've covered a lot of this throughout the chapter. You need to have strong character traits. You need to be courageous. You must have high integrity. Missing the mark in any of these areas will prevent you from leading with consistency. Remember, consistent leaders practice what they preach. They don't ask of others anything they wouldn't be willing to do themselves. They live, teach, and act as ambassadors to the values of the team and organization.

ENDURANCE

Endurance is one of the most difficult disciplines, but it is
to the one who endures that the final victory comes.

—Buddha

Early in my career, I had the privilege of working with many great
management consultants. Doug was one of my first professional
mentors. He quickly took me under his wing when I joined his consulting firm. Doug was a thirty-year veteran of the leadership and
management consulting field. He had served in many different roles
during his tenure at the firm. One thing I respected about him right
away was that he always maintained a long-term perspective on any
goal he set for himself and others. Doug was persistent under adversity and setbacks while always keeping his eye on the prize.

I can vividly remember the first consultant engagement I got to
work on with Doug. We were doing a CEO Succession project for
a midsize consumer products company. It was early in my career, so
there was a lot I needed to learn. The night before our first meeting
with the CHRO, Doug sat me down at dinner and asked a series of
questions about my background and my perspectives on the type
of consultant I wanted to be. Specifically, what would be my value
add to clients. He used this information to help me begin to shape
my brand as a management consultant. After discussing my background, Doug readily shifted attention from strategic to tactical
issues as it pertained to the engagement. He mapped out how we
would approach the initial conversations with the CEO and CHRO.
He walked me through the interview protocol for the conversations
we would have with each of the board members. He outlined the

engagement from start to finish in a clear and concise manner. He brought an energy and excitement to the project.

Doug had an incredible knack for playing at the right level with clients. He could spend the morning with the CEO and fully engage the client in the discussion. That afternoon, he could be out on the factory floor and make connections with the assembly line workers. He had a way of connecting with people and establishing rapport. Doug was skilled at quickly getting to the underlying psychology and makeup of his clients and then leveraging this information to drive impact. I saw him do this time and time again with different stakeholders.

As I got to know Doug on a deeper level, I was amazed at his perseverance and endurance. He thrived in spite of obstacles and adversity. He knew how to develop effective strategies and coping mechanisms for managing pressure and stress. This was related to the work he did inside and outside the firm. As an example, he was responsible for building out a CEO Succession practice for the firm. He communicated a passion for growing the business in this service area and owning the outcomes. In building the practice, he took the lead on the key initiatives. He was effective in delegating responsibilities to other team members so that we could maximize our efforts. He empowered others to own decisions and create intellectual property that would support the growth of the CEO Succession service area. It was not an easy task to bring an entire management consulting firm up to speed with a brand-new service offerings. Doug did this with poise and grace. He anticipated and mitigated concerns from colleagues. He created a culture where people were genuinely interested in learning and leveraging the products and services in the CEO Succession offering.

Now, although Doug seemed to have it all together on the outside, he struggled with some areas in his personal life. When I met him, he was already on his third marriage. However, no matter what was going on personally, he always brought his A-game to work. I never saw him mix his work with his personal life. He was the epitome of professionalism as a management psychologist and leadership advisory consultant.

I learned three valuable lessons from Doug. First, as management consultants, we always must look the part. From appearance to verbal and nonverbal behaviors, our knowledge and expertise in the way we come across to clients is critical. Doug taught me how to show up in a room with different clients, how to balance influence with partnership, and how to drive impact that led to repeat business and referrals. Second, he showed me that working with clients is a long-term game. You must always be mindful of where the next piece of work could come from. This was not scope creep. It was truly understanding clients' needs and anticipating how those needs would evolve over time. Third, he taught me how to have swagger as a consultant. Clients hire us for our expertise, but there is a fine balance between confidence and arrogance. Doug taught me how to walk that line. He helped me hone the skills needed to be the expert in the room, but showed me how to influence people without authority or positional power.

Doug had endurance. He knew how to maintain a long-term perspective on anything he touched. He was persistent under adversity, challenges, and setbacks. He was skilled at prioritizing the right objectives and delegating responsibilities to others as needed. He empowered those he worked with, which enabled the team to get to outcomes quicker than he could doing it all alone. It was one of my greatest professional pleasures to work with and learn from Doug. He embodied the characteristics of an enduring and battle-tested leader.

The Four Keys of Endurance

Leaders who maintain their resilience, stamina, and tenacity to achieve goals practice certain behaviors. These behaviors enable them to remain persistent under adversity and setbacks. They help them to push people past challenges and manage pressure and stress. Learning to practice the four behaviors outlined in this chapter can help any leader strengthen their endurance. It enables leaders to navigate through challenging and difficult circumstances. Whether they are leading through a crisis and uncertain times or striving to attain long-term strategic objectives, leaders who put these behaviors together achieve their desired outcomes.

Pragmatic goals

Leading with endurance is about setting the right goals. Setting practical and pragmatic goals is the best way to drive persistent focus on what matters most. When leaders set goals that are truly attainable, they set the stage for sustained effort and excellence. I've worked with many leaders who understand this principle at their core. They bring their teams together to solicit input and ideas and then identify goals that can be achieved within a reasonable time frame.

When challenges with endurance surface, it almost always has to do with unrealistic objectives. I remember working with a new CEO for a high-tech company. They were a start-up, and he had many goals he wanted the company to focus on at one point in time. We talked through the key areas and tried to highlight the top priorities. Although we had a good list of objectives put together, he wanted to go after all the items on the list. He had about eight to ten goals that the company had to accomplish over the next year. This was unrealistic. He needed to focus on the top two or three priorities and focus his team's efforts on those mission critical areas.

Going against my counsel, he decided to provide his leadership team with marching orders across all ten categories. His goals were overly ambitious and not based in the reality of where their business was today. Six months into their work, several leaders started to burn out, and their teams began to underperform due to the unrealistic objectives that were set before them. After several of the projects failed, the CEO had to scale back the organization's key objectives. They accomplished much more while enduring challenging periods because realistic goals were in place for each of his direct reports.

Playing at the right level: The power of delegation

Leaders who endure know how to play at the right level. They delegate responsibilities to team members to maximize efforts toward goal attainment. This frees up their capacity to focus on broader, strategic imperatives for the organization. It also empowers direct reports to make and own decisions within their area of responsibility.

The power of delegation is most easily recognized in seasoned leaders. They understand that they cannot do everything on their own. They must rely on the efforts of others. The best delegators know what they do well and understand the strengths and capabilities of their people. They aren't afraid to share the spotlight and understand that the team and the organization perform the best when all people are making valuable contributions.

To play at the right level requires a degree of vulnerability. You must identify your gaps and make sure there are others on the team with strengths in your areas of weakness. Some leaders struggle with this. They want to be the expert in all things. This never works with endurance. Leaders need effective strategies for managing high-pressure, high-intensity situations. Doing it all on their own can cause leaders to buckle under the stress and pressure. Prioritizing objectives and leveraging the skills of others enables leaders to achieve the most productive results.

In working with many executives across industries, I have seen firsthand the power of delegation and empowerment. Many of these leaders, especially those in sales and marketing, must manage multiple product lines while looking to grow the business. They cannot do it all on their own. They cannot be in the details all the time. They must trust in their lieutenants and let others shoulder the workload. When leaders are most effective at driving the business, they are leveraging all the human capital resources at their disposal.

Persistence

Endurance is about leading with unwavering persistence. It takes dedication and persistence to make it through challenging times. Difficult periods can occur because of the external market, competition, or internal processes and procedures (e.g., delays in product development, manufacturing issues). When these inevitable situations take place, strong leaders are persistent. They rally the troops behind a commitment to delivering on expectations and practice consistent actions and behaviors. When leaders experience setbacks, they can respond in one of two ways. Some will fold under the pressure and stress. They will have difficulty rebounding from failures or disappointments. Others will cultivate effective strategies and leverage the appropriate resources to effectively cope with adversity. I've worked with leaders on both sides of the equation.

Recently, I was coaching a pharmaceutical sales executive, and it became evident relatively quickly that he struggled with persistence. He had not experienced much adversity early in his career as he moved up the ranks and was promoted into a VP of Sales. However, once he assumed the new role, challenges started to surface. R&D was behind in the development for a new product launch. Marketing had moved too fast on launching the new product campaign. My client was stuck in the middle having to tell customers that they were going to miss their initial delivery target dates. This threw my client for a loop. He could not cope with the high-pressure, high-stress situation that he now had to deal with. We tried to work on some stress management techniques in our coaching sessions, but it did not help. Several months later, he asked to step back into a sales director role as he did not want to handle the added stress to his professional and personal life.

I've also worked with clients who thrive under pressure. They are consistently persistent despite what is going on around them. One executive who stands out was a client I coached in the retail industry. She had a passion for exceeding expectations and delivering on her commitments. Our coaching engagement took place during her company's third and fourth quarters. Fourth quarter was their highest revenue generating period. However, the retail environment was having an off year due to the economy. Her team had a huge margin to cover in revenue during the fourth quarter, and it was going to be difficult to achieve their sales goals. Despite all the struggles that her team had to endure, she kept persisting through the turbulent times. She continued to inspire her people to strive for their best every day. She remained positive and optimistic even when the weekly numbers did not look good. This galvanized her sales force. It made people want to do all they could to close more sales. At the end of the holiday season, her team did not hit their goals, but they came close (90 percent to plan). This was a testament to her ability to lead with endurance. Persistent leaders create cultures where people are decisive about the things that need to be accomplished, instead of waiting for others to provide ongoing direction. They help people get to the root cause of issues and find solutions when problems surface.

Balancing strategic and tactical issues

Endurance requires a careful balance between navigating strategic and tactical issues. Strong leaders know when to operate at a high level and when to dive into the details. They leverage the resources available to them and make productive and proficient decisions. They are ahead of the curve in anticipating and mitigating operational issues. They prioritize issues facing the organization on the most critical levers.

In many of my executive coaching engagements, the issues of strategy versus tactics regularly comes up. I typically see this with many high potentials. They quickly move up the ranks through hard work, intelligence, and a passionate commitment to excellence. However, when they get into more senior roles, they struggle with operating at an enterprise level. They tend to resort back to doing, rather than overseeing the efforts of others. They have trouble getting out of the tactical and managing at a strategic level. In one consulting engagement, I was asked to coach a rising star in a sales organization for a medical devices company. He had been one of the elite performers at an individual contributor level. He did exceptionally well as a manager of twelve sales reps for two years. He was promoted into a director level position when I began working with him. It became apparent relatively quickly that he struggled with managing his four regional managers. Part of this was because their numbers were down from the previous year. Rather than continuing to lead at a strategic level, my client felt the need to dive in on a regular basis with his regional managers. He had difficulty elevating his thinking from that of a manager to a director. We had to work on strategies for delegation, empowerment, and avoiding the tactical day-to-day management of the business. It took us several months, but my client began to consistently lead at a higher level than he did when he first took the role.

I've also worked with clients where the challenges of balancing strategic with the tactical can become too overbearing. I remember one client in the hospitality industry who was promoted from vice president (VP) to senior vice president (SVP) too quickly. He had completed several 360s over his career with his organization. In each assessment, he received low scores around delegation. However, he was a people leader with a track record of strong performance over many years. When we started our coaching work, we quickly addressed the elephant in the room—why did he have difficulty delegating and empowering his team?

As we went through his work history and leadership experiences, it quickly became clear that he was a perfectionist. Early in his career, as an individual contributor, he prided himself on delivering results and exceeding performance expectations. As he moved into management, the same drive for excellence pushed him forward. This is where he started taking on more than his people and began having trouble with delegation. He knew that this behavior had to change if he was going to be an effective SVP. We put delegation into his personal development plan and started focusing on it in our coaching sessions. We worked together for six months, but he continued to have difficulty delegating. This had a negative impact on his performance as an SVP. After several negative performance reviews, my client had to step back into a VP role, given the challenge he had around delegation. We continue to work together, and I have seen him make some progress. Hopefully, he will be able to get back to the SVPs ranks in the future.

Action Steps for Leading with Endurance

Strengthen your resolve

Endurance is about resilience. It is the ability to roll with the punches. When stress, adversity, or challenges surface, you must push through them and keep striving for your desired outcomes. When you have resilience, you harness inner strength that helps you rebound from setbacks. Although resilience won't make your problems go away, it will give you the ability to see past them. This will help you reach your goals.

The best way to strengthen your resolve is through experience. Some of my most successful clients have the unique ability to learn from experiences, both positive and negative. When a client can navigate and work through adversity, they start to strengthen the muscles needed to handle future obstacles and setbacks. When looking back through your own experiences, what obstacles and challenges have you overcome? Were you part of a turnaround in the business? Did you have to work through a poor performing sales cycle? Did you have to work with a problem employee or colleague? Take inventory, but also identify the lessons learned from those experiences.

I will never forget the first CEO whom I worked with. Lewis was identified as a rising star and high-potential leader long before he stepped into the CEO role. He was identified early through a thorough succession planning process. As a result, he was positioned for different roles across all lines of the business. My relationship with him started when he was leading sales and marketing for his organization. Lewis had to work through two acquisitions and merging two different organizational cultures. He added six new leaders to his direct report team over an eighteen-month period. He had to get his team through several quarters of poor performance. This all took place the first two years in his role. Midway through year three, he was promoted to EVP for manufacturing and R&D, a completely new role on a different side of the business. We leveraged his lessons learned from the sales and marketing experience and transferred the necessary skills to his new role. As EVP for manufacturing and R&D, Lewis lead three new product launches, opened two new manufacturing plants (one in North America and one in South America), and had to work through a product recall. These were all new challenges, and he had to have the resolve and fortitude to work through them.

After two years in this role, Lewis was promoted to EVP and general manager for the international business. He had fourteen country managers reporting into him. He was responsible for developing the two-to-three-year strategy for the international business, specifically within the emerging markets. In this role, there was a multitude of challenges that Lewis had to work through. We worked on his stamina and resilience. We handled these issues by going back to all the successes he had in his previous roles. He leveraged the insights and learning from those experiences. It helped him manage and lead the international business to three years of profitable growth. My coaching relationship with Lewis now spanned seven years in three different roles. As the board planned for CEO Succession, Lewis was identified as one of the internal succession candidates. As we prepared him for his CEO assessment process, we went back through his career to identify the lessons learned. His experiences shaped his leadership style and the way he conducted business. This helped him through the assessment process, and ultimately, he was identified as the next CEO for the organization. It was his resilience and fortitude through each of his roles that helped prepare for the CEO role.

Look for inspiration

Inspiration is all around us. Every day, we see people who deal with situations far more difficult than our own. They persevere through the challenges. Always be on the lookout for people or experiences that provide hope. Look for things that spark your energy and enthusiasm. I recommend all my clients to find some outlets for volunteer work or giving back. This opens the door for inspiration and connects us to things outside our typical sphere of influence. Many of my clients sit on nonprofit boards, and many of the organizations they oversee have tremendously strong social responsibility causes. They get to play a role in social issues, environmental issues, and all kinds of other endeavors to better their communities.

When helping clients determine how to give back, I usually ask a series of questions to point them in the right direction: What are you most passionate about outside of your work? Do you volunteer in your church or place of worship? Are you committed to pursuing social and/or political issues? Do you enjoy helping those in need? Do you love to work with children? Find out where your passions are, and you will find out where to give back. Next, what role do you want to play in your service to others? Do you want to sit on the board for your local museum? Do you want to become an active alumni from your college or university? Do you want to get on the front lines and help with hunger or poverty? Do you want to get involved at an animal shelter? Figure out the different types of ways that you can give back and then go pursue those interests. Lastly, what is your commitment to your volunteer efforts? Do you make them the lowest on the list of priorities? Are you quick to drop these pursuits when work gets hectic and busy? Do you have a network of colleagues or friends who volunteer with you and can encourage to remain committed?

The biggest challenge that executives have when giving back is finding the time. Make it a priority to find the time. I promise you it will help you appreciate the things you have and give you inspiration outside your regular day-to-day activities. When leaders maintain a balance between work and nonwork activities, they strengthen their endurance. They learn to appreciate others who find ways to persevere through difficult life circumstances.

Push through obstacles

When you're pursuing your dreams, challenges will inevitably surface. Push through these barriers. If you can't do it alone, get help. Find people who have faced similar obstacles, and seek their guidance and counsel. I always advise my clients to find mentors and role models in all areas of their life. If they want to get in better shape, find a personal trainer. If they want to get better at their finances, find a financial planner. If they want to get better at their craft, find a good mentor. If they want more insight into their leadership and personal capabilities, find a good executive coach.

Many of my clients are good at taking the first step toward getting the support that they need. They will identify a coach, mentor, or trainer to begin the process of personal development. I see them run into trouble with accountability and consistency. I remember working with a client a few years back who was eager to lose some weight and get into better shape. He was going to be celebrating his twentieth wedding anniversary later in the year. He wanted to take his wife on an exciting hiking trip to the Grand Canyon. As a couple, they used to be very active together, but as the demands of work increased, he had let the running and workouts take a backseat. The only problem was that his wife never stopped her active workout lifestyle. My client was scared he would not be able to keep up with her if they went on the hiking getaway. So we discussed how he might incorporate a workout regimen back into his busy schedule. I recommended that he get a personal trainer or, at least, an accountability partner to get him back on track. He felt he could get back into running on his own and decided not to go that route.

The first several weeks were a challenge, but we tracked his progress for the first month. Demands of work continued to persist, but he pushed through the adversity. He wasn't consistent at first. However, he started to find time each day, even for twenty to thirty minutes, to step away from the office and focus on his health. I admired the energy and effort he put toward achieving his goal. Three months into his training, he started feeling a lot better, had lost fifteen pounds, and was starting to get excited for planning the trip. In the end, he lost thirty pounds and had an amazing hiking vacation with his wife for their anniversary. His ability to persevere and endure through the first several months of training while balancing all his other responsibilities was admirable. It even inspired his children to start getting back into shape!

Always keep your eyes on the prize

Having an overarching goal or objective to accomplish is always critical to strengthening your resolve and endurance. This goes back to our chapter on vision. You must start out with an idea of what you want your desired end state to be. I've seen this happen over and over again in my consulting practice but also in my personal life. A few years back, I decided to purchase a set of golf clubs and take up the sport. How hard could it be right? I've been an athlete my whole life. I played basketball in high school and college. I was a marathon runner in my late 20s, and took up weight training and cross-fit in my thirties. I thought learning a new sport like golf would be so easy. Wow, was I wrong! Golf is not a game of power, strength, and pure athletic ability. It is about tempo, timing, balance, and consistency. I didn't know that when I picked up my first club. The one thing I did do, which I recommend to all my clients if they want to grow in any area, is get a coach.

About a week or so after I purchased my bag, I went to a driving range and took my first lesson with Tom. Tom was a seasoned PGA professional. He had worked with clients for over twenty years and was exceptionally skilled at his craft. I remember walking into my first lesson in full golf attire swag. I had on my Tiger Woods hat and matching shirt. My white pants and matching white golf shoes. You would think I was the twenty-year golfing veteran. We started hitting balls, and each of my shots went about twenty to thirty feet! It was such a humbling experience and challenged the way I looked at myself as an athlete. Everything I thought I knew about power, strength, and hand-eye coordination didn't matter with golf. You had to approach the game differently.

At the end of our first session, Tom asked me what my golf goals were. This question was a surprise at first. Golf goals? I just wanted to take out my driver and hit the ball three hundred yards! I didn't even know how to respond when he first asked the question. We talked further, and Tom explained that golf is a game of consistency. He told me that I would need to put in the time to work on my golf swing. It would require a lot of time if I wanted to improve. To do that, I needed to identify my desired end state. Did I want to be a recreational golfer? Did I want to play golf with my clients? Did I want to play golf competitively? In identifying my goal, it would give me purpose when I practiced. It would serve as a driving force in putting in the necessary work to improve. It would help me endure the challenging and frustrating periods when I felt my golf swing was making no improvements. I set my goal with Tom that very first session. It has served as a guiding force in how I practice and play the game today. Goals push you forward. They help you get through the difficult times. Always keep your main objective front and center in your thinking. This will give you purpose. It will strengthen your resolve and commitment. It will help you overcome challenges along the way. It will enable you to put in the necessary work needed to be successful in anything you do.

COMPASSION

The purpose of human life is to serve, and to show
compassion and the will to help others.
—Albert Schweitzer

My consulting firm does a lot of work with nonprofit organizations. A large component of our nonprofit portfolio is with churches and faith-based organizations. Now the church world has changed dramatically over the last twenty to twenty-five years. There has been a seismic shift from traditional denominational (e.g., Catholic, Baptist, Presbyterian) churches to nondenominational, Bible-based churches. Mega-churches like Bishop T. D. Jakes's the Potter's House or Steven Furtick's Elevation Church have thrived across the country. The idea behind many of these churches is to set up, what they call, a main campus and then open up satellite campuses. In New Jersey, where my family resides, one of the fastest-growing nondenominational churches is Hillsong Church. Founded in Australia by their senior pastor, Brian Houston, the church has grown to one of the largest churches around the world.

The US east senior pastors have a vision for opening up new campuses across the northeast. They have their main campus in New York City and have opened sites in Montclair, New Jersey; Boston, Massachusetts, and in Norwalk, Connecticut. I am a member of the church and have had the opportunity to witness firsthand their growth and expansion. I've seen that leadership is critical to the success of any church. In order to open a new campus each year, leaders must be groomed. Leadership development becomes a key priority before sending a new leadership team to a different site.

Prior to joining Hillsong Church, I worked with a senior pastor of a nondenominational church down the Jersey Shore. I met the church's senior leader, Pastor Dennis, shortly before the holiday season a few years ago. Like so many of his colleagues, Dennis had a vision for planting and growing churches. As I began to learn more about Dennis and his vision for the future, it became clear that his team needed leadership development. If his church was to begin moving to a multisite model, he would need to create a culture of leadership and leadership development. I started coaching Dennis, and we outlined a plan to develop a leadership competency model for his staff. From this, we would design and implement a leadership development program for his high-potential leaders—those he identified and selected to open new church sites. As I got to learn more about Pastor Dennis, I quickly came to understand his values and beliefs. He lived by two mottos: love people, and relationships are everything. He had a positive impact on people through his communication, social awareness, and relational intelligence.

As we began to develop a leadership competency model for his staff, I witnessed his leadership in action. He built trust by being open with communication, demonstrating empathy, and sharing information. We discussed his ideas for what a good church leader should look like, but he wanted to take things a step further. He valued the opinions of his staff, and so we developed a first draft of key leadership competencies. He shared with his entire leadership team. This created a sense of ownership on the part of his people. It also helped church leaders start to think with a leadership mindset.

Once we had their leadership competency model in place, we began the process of identifying talent. Through this process, I got to see how Pastor Dennis connected with people. I saw his compassion for others. He had a great sense of what people were good at (their gifts) and placed people in roles where they would succeed. He empathized with the experience of others and did not overly rely on his personal experiences when building teams. I saw him mentor and develop people with an eye toward the future. This took a lot of his time. Some would argue that the lead pastor must focus more on vision and strategy than on people and relationships. I've seen many pastors that do this. They surround themselves with the "touchy-feely" folks who can build people up. Pastor Dennis was not like this. He placed such a strong emphasis on relationships that it impacted everything he did.

Pastor Dennis would have weekly one-on-ones with his key direct reports. These were not check-in conversations. They were about compassionately supporting his people. He strived to serve others. This engendered loyalty, trust, and commitment from his people. The amazing thing was that almost all of his staff were volunteers. No one was paid for their efforts. As an example, his worship leader was there every Sunday at 6:00 a.m. to set up the musical instruments and practice with his team. This leader never missed a Sunday! It's a testament to the relationship Pastor Dennis built with all of his leaders.

He was also a great listener. I assumed this was something that all pastors needed to do, but Pastor Dennis took it to a whole different level. From the first-time guest to a loyal church goer for years, he made personal connections with people from all walks of life. He also had the ability to possess a deep understanding of others and an ability to anticipate their needs. He knew if folks were having a bad day or a rough week. He wanted people to grow in their relationships with God. He modeled this love and compassion for people in all that he did. As we designed and rolled out the leadership development program, I saw him take a lead role in making sure the program was a success. He didn't have to do this. He could have delegated it to other folks in the church. This was simply another testament to his commitment to people. He wanted deep, personal relationships with all of his leaders. This was especially true for the new and emerging staff. I greatly admire Pastor Dennis for his steadfast commitment to people and relationships. He is one of the rare leaders who is skilled at building rapport, embracing individual differences, developing trust, and cultivating influence. These four skills are critical to successfully building and sustaining long-term relationships.

Why Compassion Matters

There is no clearer showcase of your character than in your relationships. By nature, we all want to connect and feel appreciated by others. Good leaders understand this principle and lead with compassion. They know how to impact people through effective communication, social awareness, and relational intelligence. Some of the best leaders whom I have worked with strive toward building strong and lasting relationships with others. They take the time needed on the front-end to learn about people—what makes them tick, their interests and ambitions, and their talents and capabilities. When I've seen leaders put in the time to build relationships, the alignment, buy-in, commitment, and loyalty from their people is astonishing.

Several years back, I began working with a bank in the Bahamas. The organization hired us to help them find a successor to their founder and CEO. The founder wanted a leader who valued relationships and put people first. We assessed many candidates, but it took a while to find a leader with the right mix of social and emotional intelligence—the type of leader who would put the greatest emphasis on the bank's most important assets, their people. After a three- to four-month period, we met Marcus. He was a leader in the industry with the breadth and depth of experience needed to see the next phase of the organization's growth. He possessed many talents, but his greatest assets were his compassion and dedication to people.

After assessing Marcus, I began working with him as his executive onboarding and integration coach. In our first session, Marcus and I talked through how he could gain the greatest traction with his teams. We focused on his leadership team first. He wanted to introduce new cultural pillars and leadership competencies that would inspire and galvanize the organization. To do this, he first took time to build relationships with each of his direct reports. These were not surface-level connections. He went out of his way the first several months to invest in those relationships. He had weekly one-on-ones with each of his people. He took time to learn about their backgrounds and stories. He shared his story. He learned about their goals and ambitions; the legacy and impact they wanted to have on the organization. I was impressed at how much time he invested in getting to know his team. It didn't stop with his direct reports, though. He wanted to establish a foundation of buy-in and commitment from leaders at all levels of the firm.

After building his initial connections with his leadership team, he then went on to establishing relationships with all the functions across the firm. He took time to learn about the people and teams in finance, operations, HR, IT, and marketing. He made sure to meet with every employee. He was honest, open, and empathetic toward everyone. Once he made it through the corporate functions, he went on to each of their branches across the islands to build relationships with the branch managers and their teams. Within a six-month time frame, he had met with over three quarters of the bank's employee population. His commitment to relationships and showing compassion toward others garnered loyalty and commitment from his employees. Marcus believed in the best about people. He understood that nothing could be accomplished unless he took the time to invest in people. The bank is thriving today because of the strong emphasis Marcus places on people and the relationships he has built with leaders across the firm.

Laying the Foundation:
The Need for Social and Emotional Intelligence

Compassionate leaders have good social and emotional intelligence. They know how to leverage and monitor their own emotions and are perceptive to the emotions and feelings of others. I've spent most of my career studying emotional intelligence (EQ). Since I was an undergraduate at Fairleigh Dickinson University, I was fascinated by the concept of EQ. When I was a freshman, I picked up Daniel Goleman's book *Emotional Intelligence*, and it changed the way I looked at communicating with others. Goleman defined EQ as the capability of people to recognize their own emotions and those of others, discern between different feelings and label them appropriately, use emotional information to guide thinking and behavior, and manage and/or adjust emotions to adapt to environments or achieve goals. Some of the most effective leaders I have had the privilege of working with understand the power of emotional intelligence. They are able to read situations and people, understand moods and emotions, and communicate in ways that express empathy and authenticity.

I regularly use EQ in my coaching work with clients. One of my clients in the telecommunication space was exceptionally skilled at leveraging EQ. In our first coaching session, John talked, at length, about the importance of the connections and relationships he had with others. In almost every situation he described, he outlined how he used EQ to build stronger connections with colleagues. We started working together when he was promoted to a vice president of sales. He wanted to build a high-caliber leadership team, so we mapped out the steps that would be needed to do that. He would need to understand each of his regional sales managers as well as their district management teams. To do this, he spent the first six months learning all he could about his people. He didn't just learn about how they ran their businesses; he invested the time to learn about each of his leaders individually.

I also found John to have exceptional self-awareness, a critical foundational component of EQ. He understood his strengths and opportunities, the impact he had on others, and how to galvanize people around a vision. He was also skilled at self-regulation. He was a passionate and fiery leader but understood how to control his impulses and manage his emotions effectively. I remember sitting in one of his staff meetings when one of his direct reports was complaining about their people. The regional manager was relentless in bashing their team and how they were missing their sales goal targets. Rather than get caught up in the moment, John diffused the situation by coaching his direct report on what they could do to turn things around. He focused on brainstorming and resolving the problem rather than impulsively talking down or criticizing his direct report. John's use of EQ didn't end with his team. One of our coaching goals was strengthening the relationships he had with peers and senior management. Again, I saw John leverage his ability to understand others and use his understanding of emotions to cultivate strong partnerships with others.

Leaders who possess high EQ are usually effective at getting things done through others. Not only are they good at understanding their emotions and the emotions of others; they are skilled at using social intelligence. Goleman's second book on relationships, *Social Intelligence*, took a deeper dive into the power of the connections we have with others. He defines social intelligence (SI) as the ability to get along with others and to get people to cooperate with one's goals and objectives. SI focuses on one's ability to have social awareness—understanding the dynamics that govern social interactions. Leaders who have high SI have a depth of knowledge and experience with different interactions styles and strategies that can be used to influence others. They are able to use verbal and nonverbal cues to elicit positive responses from people. They understand social roles, customs, and idiosyncrasies that govern the way people and teams operate. They have exceptional listening skills. They have strong impression management—presenting oneself in a way that connects with others—capabilities.

Some of the most socially intelligent leaders I have worked with have a knack for making people feel valued and appreciated. About six years ago, I worked with a CEO of an insurance company that embodied high emotional and social intelligence. William made people feel warm and welcome when he interacted with them. He took time to learn people's stories and always made sure to talk about more than just work. He did simple things like ask how one's spouse or kids were doing. He invested time in helping people grow and develop. I never saw him walk away from a conversation where he could provide career guidance and support to others. He even practiced this with leaders one or two levels below the c-suite. As I got to know William deeper, I began to see that there was more behind his EQ and SI skills. He genuinely cared about people. He wanted the best for leaders across his organization. He showed compassion and understanding to all he worked with. This wasn't a front or some way to influence them to produce more. He believed in his people and their potential. In my twenty years of coaching leaders, I never saw someone more authentic than William. Through our coaching work, I started to realize that his connections with people went deeper than emotional and social intelligence. He had compassion for others. His compassion was expressed in deeper connections and relationships that he built with his people. These connections were developed through his use of what I call relational intelligence.

Relational Intelligence

During my graduate studies, I developed a passion for studying relationships and the power they have on employee performance and productivity. Although there was a litany of research on emotional and social intelligence, I knew something was missing. How did some leaders build exceptional relationships with others? What behaviors did they practice? What did they do specifically to garner so much trust, buy-in, and support from their people? My curiosity with these questions led me to write my dissertation on the concept of relational intelligence. I define relational intelligence as one's ability to build and maintain long-term connections and partnerships with others. Relationally intelligent leaders know how to establish rapport. They take time to learn and understand about the talent and capabilities of others. They embrace individual differenced with people. They are skilled at developing trust. They cultivate influence through their ability to empower and inspire people. Leaders who apply these behaviors and skills are able to bring out the best in others.

Establishing rapport

The foundation of any lasting and sustainable relationship starts with establishing rapport. Leaders who take the time to build rapport understand the importance of connecting with people. I define *rapport building* as the process of beginning a relationship of mutual trust, harmony, and understanding. Rapport is often viewed as a starting point for developing trust and influence with others by using empathy and respect to create an environment of mutual understanding. Research in the business psychology community has found that leaders who take time to build rapport are skilled at developing and using diverse networks. They understand the value of making people feel welcome and appreciated. I have seen this behavior in action with many of my clients. The clients that do it the best look for opportunities to relate to others.

I do a lot of work in the restaurant hospitality industry and have worked with many small business owners. Several years ago, I worked with a small business owner named Maria who had several restaurants in the New York/New Jersey region. She had been in the restaurant industry for over twenty years and was exceptional at hiring people who knew how to connect with others. I was brought in to build a leadership development program for her general managers. As part of my due diligence discovery work, I interviewed staff from all of her locations. Most of the bartenders I spoke with exceled at establishing rapport with customers.

During one of my visits, I remember interviewing a bartender who was one of Maria's high performers. We talked about her role, the culture of the restaurant, and the experience they try to give to their customers. What stood out to me was how she established rapport with others. She explained to me how she always used verbal and nonverbal cues to make patrons feel warm and welcomed. She wasn't overly assertive if a customer wasn't talkative but was persistent in making the connection. She was quick to identify social cues or indications of why the customer might be at the restaurant that night. Were they just finishing up with work and needed to relax? Were they waiting for friends or going on a date? Were they there for a family party? Depending on her hypothesis of the situation, she would adjust her approach to fit the moment.

She was always quick to compliment people. She didn't do this to get a good tip. It was a way to engage a person in conversation. This would usually break the ice and give her a place to find common ground. Not only did she initiate the dialogue, but she was consistent in using nonverbal cues to draw her customers in. She smiled and made eye contact during interactions. She leaned into a conversation and made each customer feel like they were the only one at the bar.

She was also curious, asking questions to learn about others. She used humor to lighten the mood. She was a firm believer in treating people how she would want to be treated if she was out at a restaurant. It was no wonder she had many repeat customers. People were drawn to her because of the connections she built with them.

Through my years of coaching and consulting with clients, I have found that there are six areas that contribute to establishing rapport. First, there needs to be some form of similarity between two people. Do they share something in common—cultural norms and values, personal beliefs, environmental influences, personalities, attitudes, or experiences? Second, there needs to be some type of interest or reason in getting to know one another. In the workplace, this can be as simple as working together on the same project or initiative. Third, each individual has to have good self-awareness. How are they coming across to the other person? Are they aware of the social cues in the conversation? Do they know when to talk and when to listen? Fourth, there needs to be a good awareness of the other individual. How are they responding? Are they engaged in the conversation? Do they want to continue the dialogue? Fifth, they need to be aware of the types of words they use in the conversation. Are they using words that are brash and abrasive? Are they using words that are friendly and cordial? Lastly, they need to use the right nonverbal behaviors—the use of signals like their physical appearance, the way they dress, eye contact, posture, hand gestures, and proximity to the other person.

Establishing rapport is the foundational skill in developing one's relational intelligence. Leaders who know how to establish rapport lay the groundwork for long-term positive relationships. Once a leader builds an initial connection with others, they need to dive deeper. They need to figure out what makes others tick. They need to identify people's talents, interests, and capabilities. They need to understand the strengths and areas of opportunities of their people. To do this, they must take time to practice the second skill of relational intelligence—taking time to understand others and embrace individual differences.

Understanding others and embracing individual differences

Leaders get the most out of their employees when they take time to develop a deep understanding about them. This goes beyond having an awareness of the emotions and feelings of others. It is about taking the time to learn about people's backgrounds, experiences, interests, and capabilities. I define *understanding others and embracing individual differences* as the ability to develop a favorable reception and opinion toward other people or situations that are different from one's culture, background, and experiences. It is a critical component of relational intelligence because it allows leaders to understand how others are wired and what truly motivates them. Studies conducted in the field of business psychology have found that leaders who are skilled at understanding people (e.g., age ethnicity, gender, race, physical abilities, religious beliefs, sexual orientation, education, values and interests, and beliefs) possess higher levels of social skill and are more effective communicators.

In the last ten years, there has been a huge focus on diversity and inclusion in organizations. These types of programs speak to the vast array of talents and skills that an organization can benefit from when they have a diverse workforce. Business leaders define diversity in the workplace in many different ways. One definition emphasizes the types of group identities or characteristics that employees use to understand individual differences. Another definition focuses on the effects of demographic backgrounds on the types of exchanges between two coworkers. Regardless of the definition, a focus on diversity has positive effects on job performance, group cohesion, organizational commitment, job satisfaction, and employee morale.

I've had the opportunity to work with many leaders who place a strong emphasis on diversity and inclusion. Chris, a district manager in the retail industry, was one of the best leaders I've worked with when it comes to diversity and understanding others. We began our coaching work when he was promoted into his role. He oversaw fifteen stores in his district and had a team of twenty direct reports. Given that he was promoted from a store, he had several challenges. First, he got the promotion over four of his peers who also applied for the position. Second, he didn't have strong relationships with some of the store managers. He knew them in passing but had not had the opportunity to spend time with any of them. Third, several of his store managers were new to their roles. When we first met, we outlined a plan to address all three areas.

What I admired most about Chris was that he was fully committed to learning all he could about his people. He spent the first four months visiting each of his stores to build relationships with his leaders. He did this by having regular one-on-ones with his direct reports. In these meetings, he took time to learn about his people's backgrounds, interests, and capabilities. He didn't stop there. He wanted to learn their stories. How did their prior work experiences shape their leadership? What personal experiences helped form their values and beliefs? How did they lead their teams? What were their goals and desires for their future? He encouraged all his team members to hire people with different backgrounds. He supported them in the development of diverse leadership teams.

I saw him personally go out of his way to take time for the leaders who did not get the district manager role. He worked with each of them to develop personal goals that would prepare them for future opportunities. He also spent a great deal of time with the store managers that he did not know. He shared his values and beliefs as a leader. He outlined his vision for their stores and helped them with their professional development. For those who were new to their roles, he offered them guidance and counsel around what made a successful store. In less than a year, his team was one of the highest-performing districts in the region. I credit this to his emphasis on diversity. He had a team that was made up of different races and ethnicities. He placed a strong emphasis on growing and developing women. He recognized and rewarded leaders who built store cultures that were inclusive of their employees.

Going beyond diversity and inclusion, understanding others and embracing individual differences is about taking time to learn what people are good at and giving them opportunities to grow and develop. Leaders who take time to learn about their people are usually good at mentoring and coaching. They possess a deep understanding of, and an ability to, anticipate the needs of others through listening and observation. They can hone in on people's strengths and development opportunities and have no problem providing feedback. They create cultures of transparency by setting a positive example for others. They are candid, authentic, and compassionate, with a sincere respect and appreciation for the work of their employees. They know how to empathize with the backgrounds and experiences of different people.

Valerie, a senior vice president of marketing in the pharmaceuticals industry, was exceptional at developing her people. I assessed her for the marketing role and began coaching her shortly after she was hired. Valerie was all about people development. In our first coaching session, she told me how important it was to build a strong team. She wanted to put personal development plans in place for all her people. She felt it was her job as a servant leader to help them grow. She did this by putting in the time and energy needed to build solid relationships with each of her direct reports. She also wanted to learn all she could about their work and the way they led their teams. I was impressed that she placed such a strong emphasis on people. She did this before focusing on her goals and objectives as a marketing leader. She believed that her function would exceed performance expectations if her people felt she fully supported them.

Over the course of our work together, I came to realize how compassionate and committed she was toward her people. Several of her direct reports were promoted within the first eighteen months she was with the organization. The marketing function achieved all of its goals and key performance indicators in her first year. This was a testament to the work she put in to understand her people. However, she also did something else that is key to relational intelligence. She developed trust with all her people. It was through the trust she built individually and collectively with her people that made them such a high-performing team.

Developing trust

Leaders who develop trusting relationships get the most out of their people. They build teams and organizations where people can rely on one another to drive results. They get buy-in and support for their initiatives. They create an environment of open dialogue and honesty between employees. They are not afraid to admit when they're wrong and are quick to turn to others for guidance and support. As the third component of the relational intelligence framework, I define *developing trust* as the intention of taking a risk or exposing oneself to the actions and behaviors of another person. It is allowing yourself to be vulnerable in a situation based on the positive expectations of another's intentions. Trust is typically built when you are placed in ambiguous situations where the outcomes can have positive or negative consequences depending on the actions of others. Although positive outcomes strengthen trust, it is usually the negative outcomes that have a greater influence on the relationship between two people.

Developing trust has several important benefits to leaders and their employees. It provides the basis for enhancing interpersonal relationships without the need for continual proof of the legitimate intentions of others. At the individual and team level, studies have shown that trust is critical to productivity, group cohesion, cooperation, and performance effectiveness. At the organizational level, trust is linked to cross-functional partnerships, values and ethics, corporate alliances, and relationships to customers. Trust is also critical to the successful development of any relationship between consultants and their clients.

One of my colleagues at our firm is great at building trust with our clients. Michael builds trust in stages. After establishing rapport and developing a deep understanding of his clients' needs, he engages in behaviors that consistently put equity into the bank account of trust. It is an iterative process. I remember vividly how he did this with one of our most difficult accounts. Michael had to win over a large amount of skepticism from Tom, the CEO of a consumer products company, during the early stages of our work with their organization. Tom had worked with consulting firms before and held a biased view that consultants were too pricey and didn't really add value. The board of directors felt differently. They needed Tom to put in place a succession plan for the organization and hired us to support the initiative. In our first meeting with Tom, Michael took the lead on outlining our process and what it meant for Tom on a personal level. Tom had been CEO for five years. Legacy was most important to him as he began to focus on retirement.

Given Tom's skepticism of the process, Michael took time to invest in the relationship. He made sure to keep lines of communication open with Tom, especially in the early stages where we were having more interactions with the board. Michael had to ensure Tom felt we were on his side even though the board was our primary client in the engagement. Michael outlined our process in detail to put Tom at ease. He followed through on commitments and time lines that were established by the board. He listened to Tom's input on both the internal and external candidates we assessed. This established buy-in and alignment with Tom's expectations. It also allowed Michael to get at Tom's major underlying concern—that the right successor would be put in place to drive the company into its next phase of growth.

Over a four-month period, I watched Michael masterfully develop a strong partnership with Tom. Tom began to reach out to Michael about issues outside of the CEO succession engagement. Michael started to become Tom's trusted advisor. They developed a personal relationship over this time as well. In the end, we were successful in helping the company identify Tom's successor. Michael also became Tom's executive coach and helped shepherd Tom's transition. This happened because Michael invested the time to develop trust with his client.

When trust is not developed successfully, it damages relationships and has a negative impact on an organization. Several years back, I worked with the chief marketing officer of a clothing retailer who was new to her role. She was charismatic and engaging. People gravitated to her because of her energy and enthusiasm. As a new leader in a high-profile role, she needed to have a successful integration into the organization. At first, she took time to learn about her colleagues and invested in getting to know others. She made commitments to the CEO and her peers. She established relationships with her direct reports.

I thought she was starting to gain traction when things began to go off the rails. She started to rely on her past work experiences rather than adjust her style to fit the culture of the organization. She missed deadlines and didn't keep her commitments to the sales function. This caused a friction between her and the executive vice president of sales. He couldn't trust her to deliver on her commitments. She also began implementing certain rules of engagement for her team but didn't model the right behaviors for her people. She went behind people's backs to find out information and used it against others in team settings. People didn't trust her, and it had a huge negative impact on her team. Within eighteen months, she was let go by the company because of the damage she had caused. It was a perfect example of how a lack of trust can destroy anyone's success.

The development of trust is critical to any working relationship. When it is established, leaders thrive. They are effective in getting things done through others and build equity over time. When it is lacking, performance suffers, and people become disengaged. Leaders who build trust set the foundation for influence. They create pathways to driving success and can truly motivate and inspire others. They are able to impact the organization in ways that extend beyond their duties and responsibilities. Developing trust opens the door for cultivating influence.

Cultivating influence

Relational intelligence is about influence. Leaders who inspire and motivate others do so by influencing people's behaviors and actions. They bring people together through relationship building, understanding others, and developing trust. They understand how to influence with and without authority. I define *cultivating influence* as a leader's ability to communicate a well-devised vision for the future, build trust among colleagues, and take effective action to accomplish organizational objectives. It is about inspiring people to perform above and beyond stated expectations.

In the field of business psychology, there is a litany of research on leadership and influence. Many organizational psychologists view influence as the use of noncoercive tactics used to direct and coordinate the activities of employees toward the accomplishment of specific goals and strategic imperatives. Influence takes place primarily through the partnerships that are established between leaders and their people. The quality of the relationships that have been developed between these leaders and their employees are based on many factors (e.g., technical skills, interpersonal style, trustworthiness, and levels of sensitivity). These factors have been found to have a significant impact on support, rewards, and job satisfaction. I have also found that the influence leaders have on employees helps to build levels of self-esteem and worth. They make people feel valued for their contributions and help support the development of their talents and capabilities.

William, a senior executive in the sports and entertainment industry, was exceptional at cultivating influence with others. He did this over time by the relationships he formed with his people. This was not a one-size-fits-all approach to leadership. He adjusted his style to fit the needs, talents, and interests of each of his team members. Although he had certain personality characteristics that attracted others, he practiced certain influence skills that resonated with people. He was always friendly and engaging. People trusted that he had their best interests at heart. He took time to support people's growth. He was skilled at identifying the strengths and opportunities of his direct reports and assigned them to projects and initiatives that would showcase their talents.

I started working with William when he was getting ready to merge two functions into one team. Changes to the organization's structure required sales and marketing to become one team. This was after years of working under separate umbrellas. Sales employees were known across the company as the star performers. Marketing people were valued, but did not have the clout that the sales team had. William was responsible for bringing the two groups together and forming one collaborative culture. To do this, we outlined the steps that would be needed to get employees from both teams on the same page. He began by bringing the leadership teams of the two functions together. He outlined his vision of how the new team would operate. He listened to their issues and concerns about the transition. He established rules of engagement and norms that team members were to follow. Although these were critical factors to building alignment, he cultivated influence by connecting with each of his people on an individual level.

He started the process of understanding what each leader needed to be successful. He made himself available as a resource at all times. He modeled the right behaviors for people to follow—behaviors like practicing what he preached, putting in the extra efforts to meet deadlines, and delivering on his commitments. He lived the values of the organization and encouraged his direct reports to do the same. There were bumps in the road as resources needed to be allocated and tough decisions had to be made on talent at lower levels of the function. However, he always reinforced the importance of supporting his people. Within six months, he had built strong relationships with each of his direct reports. This united people around a shared level of commitment to their core purpose. He had cultivated influence in such a way that his people became loyal followers. His direct reports would go through walls for him because they knew he would do the same.

When leaders are effective at influencing others, there are many positive benefits to their people and to their organizations. Researchers have found that when leaders are effective in cultivating influence, it leads to many positive outcomes for their companies. Some of these outcomes include organizational commitment, job satisfaction, employee well-being, cooperation, job performance, and productivity. Leaders who excel at cultivating influence also have strong social awareness. They know how to read people and situations extremely well. They are flexible and adaptable to different situations and know how to evoke desired responses from others. They also possess high levels of emotional intelligence. They have strong self-awareness and know how to use emotions to captivate an audience and galvanize people to drive performance objectives.

Relational intelligence is the cornerstone of compassion. Leaders who take time to invest in relationships and put people first get the best out of others. Their innate ability to connect on a deep level with people fosters buy-in and commitment. It makes people feel valued, appreciated, and supported. Compassionate leaders are highly effective communicators. They know how to use emotional, social, and relational intelligence to enhance the work they do through others. They go the extra mile when it comes to understanding their people—both on a personal and professional level. They place people before themselves. They understand the power behind building deep connections with others.

Action Steps for Leading with Compassion

Sharpen your EQ

Emotional intelligence is a foundational component of compassion. Leaders with high EQ understand what makes them tick. They have put in the work to develop their self-awareness. They are reflective about their past and aware of how it has informed decisions they have made over their career. They are skilled at identifying their strengths and developmental opportunities. They are open to feedback and eager to make behavioral changes that will improve their performance. They understand when to use emotions to elicit positive responses from others. They use emotional information to guide their thinking. They are effective at managing and adjusting emotions to adapt to different environments and people.

There are many ways to develop and sharpen your EQ. One way is to partner with other leaders who are strong in this space and learn how they use emotions to engage others. What information do they use to process their emotions? How do they leverage the resources around them to adjust their emotional approach to different environments? How do they manage their emotions in times of stress or high-stakes situations? Being mentored by a leader with high EQ can help you refine your approach toward using emotions to drive positive and productive outcomes. Another way involves working with an executive coach. Through a partnership with your coach, you will be able to identify and tap into the underlying emotions that impact your behavior.

Several years ago, I was brought into an organization to work with a high-performing vice president of operations for a utilities company. He was a great people leader. He took time to develop his people and always supported their professional growth. He championed diversity and valued having people with different backgrounds and experiences on his team. He knew how to motivate and inspire others. His challenge was managing his emotions. He had such great passion for his work that when he became frustrated or agitated it would show. This happened usually with peers or cross-functional colleagues. He would be in meetings or conference calls, and if he was challenged, he would go after others. He was relentless in arguing his point of view. He was combative and defensive whenever there was a slight criticism of his work or the work of his team. If he didn't address these emotional outbursts, he was going to have great difficulty moving up in the organization.

What fascinated me was how much of a strong emphasis he placed on making sure his people developed their EQ. In partnership with his HRBP, he built training courses and curriculum on emotional intelligence that all his leaders were expected to go through. He led most of these trainings and had such a strong command on the subject. It was puzzling to me why he couldn't implement parts of what he taught others into his personal leadership repertoire. We spent many of our early coaching sessions looking to uncover why he didn't have strong impulse control. As we worked through the problem, I learned that there were many issues that had occurred early on in his life that shaped how he processed and managed his emotions. He came from a family where alcohol and drugs were regularly abused by both of his parents. He had to fend for himself most of his childhood years. There was always a chip on his shoulder. He had a fear of failure and didn't want to end up like his parents. This motivated him to be as successful as he could in his work and professional life. When he felt challenged or thought others didn't appreciate his efforts, he was quick to let his emotions get the best of him.

I had to convince him that he was an asset to the company and being challenged by others wasn't a sign that he was failing. It was simply feedback and input that he could use to improve his work and the work of his team. After several months, we were able to put into practice certain mechanisms and behavioral modifications for when he started to react out of emotion rather than logic. Given that he aspired to take on roles of greater responsibility for his company, he started to implement the right behaviors which dramatically changed the way he interacted with colleagues.

Develop your relational intelligence

Leaders who are compassionate are relationally intelligent. They know how to connect with people on a deep level. They place others before themselves. They make people feel valued and appreciated. So how does one develop relational intelligence? Is it learned over time and experience, or do people have to put the skills into practice every day? The answer is both. Some leaders are born with an affinity for people. These tend to be the charismatic type. However, all leaders can put the four relational intelligence skills into practice. It doesn't matter if you're an extrovert or an introvert. It doesn't matter if you're well networked or have a small circle of people whom you trust. What matters most is the desire to make your relationships better.

Establishing rapport is learned by practice. It is most easily practiced in job interviews, in selection and promotion processes, when new teams form, and when leaders transition into new roles. As an interviewer, you need to make sure your interviewee is as comfortable as you can. The skills we highlighted earlier in the chapter—the use of verbal and nonverbal gestures—if applied consistently put people at ease. They create an environment for open dialogue and discussion. When hiring or promoting people, rapport building is used to familiarize yourself with others. It helps you get a feel for how someone will adapt and adjust to the organization. It enables you to start to understand what makes the other person tick. When forming a new team, your ability to establish rapport can quickly get people aligned and on the same team. It helps to make your direct reports feel valued and appreciated. When transitioning into a new role, your ability to establish strong connections early on garners buy-in and support from people. It helps others get a sense of how it will be to work with you.

Understanding others, embracing individual differences, and developing trust can be practiced by asking the right questions and giving people an opportunity to demonstrate their trustworthiness. Early in my career, I experienced this with a senior colleague on my team. I remember her frequently taking time to get to know me. She would regularly stop by my office and ask questions—questions about how my work was going, how I was acclimating to the firm, and what my interests were outside of work. She offered some of her personal insights and stories as well, stories about the firm's history and the history of colleagues in our office. She gave me opportunities to partner with her when working with our clients. She took time to invest in our relationship. These behaviors made me want to learn more about her and deliver the quality of work that would make her and the firm look good. It inspired me to take time to learn about other colleagues in our office. That is the power of understanding others and developing trust. These two skills, when put into practice regularly, exemplify the qualities of a compassionate leader.

Cultivating influence is perhaps the most difficult skill to practice because you need to be proficient in the other areas before it can start to take shape. When you have established rapport, taken time to understand others, and developed trust, the groundwork for influence has been laid. Influence then enables you to get others to buy into your vision. It makes people genuinely feel that their efforts contribute to the overarching goals and objectives of the business. It lets them know that you value who they are as people and not just the work that they do. Influential leaders understand the power of relationships and do all they can to form them with their people.

Look for role models

If you want to be more compassionate in your leadership, you need to find role models who can show you the way. Role models are great because they typically practice what they preach. I am a firm believer that you can learn more by observation than you can in any classroom or training setting. So how do you identify the right role models? Do you look for people who are successful? If so, how are you defining success? Is it by identifying the people with the greatest relationships? Those with the most followers? Over my career, I have tried to surround myself with people who inspire me, with those who have capabilities that I may be lacking, and with people who genuinely put others first. They treat people the way they want to be treated. I have found this to be my formula for growth—growth as a consultant, as a leader, and as a person who truly values relationships.

I have found with many of my clients that it can be hard to find the right role models. This is especially true for those who are new to an organization. They typically look to peers and their manager as the primary support systems. This can be a tricky road to travel because not all peers are equally invested in a new hire's success. In my executive integration coaching engagements, I focus my clients on four critical stages that will drive integration success. These stages go beyond the first ninety days and focus on the first twelve to eighteen months of their tenure. Each stage requires the identification and partnership with different types of role models. For the honeymoon stage, the first one to three months in role, it is critical for new leaders to find people who are encouraging and supportive, people who are great stewards of the company's values and beliefs. These role models transmit positive, confirming messages that reinforce the mission and guiding purpose for the organization.

In the reality stage, months four through six, new leaders need to identify people who are honest and transparent. Those who can reaffirm the value the new hire brings to the organization and help offset some of the doubts one might have about joining the company. It is at this stage that cross-functional role models are important. Stage three, the adjustment phase, is where new leaders typically start to form solid relationships. They need to partner with people who are skilled in their area of expertise and can be used as a resource to help drive success. For example, a new sales leader would benefit greatly from working with their marketing counterpart. The marketing leader understands the workflow between the two functions and could help support the sales leader on acclimating to the culture.

In the final stage, full integration, new leaders typically have a strong lay of the land. Knowledge about more subtle aspects of the organization increases. New leaders begin to form personal relationships with others. They recognize that they still have a lot to learn but feel a sense of success and accomplishment. This is the most critical stage for identifying the right role models. It is here that the right role model will help support some of the different key integration success factors (e.g., networking, navigating culture, and accelerating learning).

For those who have long tenure with an organization, role models are used in different ways. For example, VPs that aspire to SVP or EVP roles may want to look for those who possess certain qualities or personal characteristics that make leaders at those levels successful. The other side of the role model equation is mentoring. When seasoned leaders take others under their wing, they help people build confidence, expose them to new opportunities, and serve as valuable sources for developmental feedback. If you're looking for a role model, look for leaders who align with your values and beliefs—those who have some similar characteristics that you do and skills that can help you learn and grow. If you're looking to mentor people and serve as a role model, look for those who have a passion for what they do. The types of people who are proactive and take initiative. This always helps strengthen commitment and loyalty to the organization. It can also be one of the most rewarding personal experiences as a leader— to help others achieve their goals maximize their potential.

Take time for others

Compassion is all about communication and relationships. The most effective leaders take time to cultivate deep, long-term partnerships with others. They place more of an emphasis on people than they do on tasks, goals, and performance objectives. In this chapter, I have outlined the way to build strong relationships with others. The foundation of social and emotional intelligence enables you to understand yourself and how to engage with others. Relational intelligence goes a step further to highlight the critical skills required to build successful relationships. However, these skills need to be put into practice to achieve positive relational outcomes. This is where it is important to have a genuine interest in getting to know the people whom you work with. You have to find ways to take the time to get to know others.

Mark, a retail executive I worked with many years ago, was exceptional at taking time to learn about his people. He believed that the best results are accomplished when people feel valued, cared for, and appreciated. I started working with him after there was a re-org, and many of his direct reports had transitioned from other parts of the business. He had a team of nine and only had prior relationships with four of those leaders. Early on in our coaching partnership, we discussed how to get the team aligned and on the same page. We talked through how he would like to leverage the talents and capabilities of each of his direct reports, but also how he would establish connections with each of them. I outlined some simple steps he could take to do this in a reasonable time frame. He needed to know how they felt about the organizational changes that had taken place. Were they frustrated by the changes? Did they have questions and concerns about how things would be under his leadership? What were their goals and desires moving forward? What were their strengths and developmental opportunities? What motivated and inspired each of them?

He could have gone about finding this information in a very direct and transactional manner. However, that was not Mark's style. He took time to meet each of his people individually and did it in a variety of ways. Some he took out to lunch and dinner. Others he traveled with to their stores and facilities. Some he invited to special events and meetings with senior executives. He found ways to learn about each of his leaders and get at the underlying questions above. I was amazed at how quickly he was able to find common ground with each of his direct reports. The effort he invested early on in each of the relationships paid huge dividends down the road. The team was more aligned, people understood their roles and responsibilities, and there was commitment to their shared vision for the future. Had Mark been very scripted in his approach and treated each leader the same, he wouldn't have gotten the buy-in that he needed.

As you think through the different relationships in your workplace, make sure you are taking time to get to know others. This applies to new hires as well as seasoned employees. The more time you take to get to know others, the more they will be committed to you. You have to invest in getting to know people if you want to build camaraderie, create a solid and stable foundation of trust, and maximize potential. It will also be extremely rewarding when you feel that deep connection with others. One of the most gratifying parts of my consulting work is when I have built strong, long-term relationships with my clients. It has helped me to understand how I can impact people on a deep level. It has given me a window into how people think and what's most important to them on a personal and professional level. It has also strengthened me as a consultant. No two relationships are the same. Just because leaders may have the same title or similar responsibilities in an organization, we all are different. We all bring a unique perspective based on diverse life experiences that shape how we view the world. When you take time to get to know others and build relationships, you get a glimpse into people's worlds. It is the best way to help others achieve their hopes, goals, and dreams.

INSPIRATION

Inspiration and genius—one and the same.
                                        —Victor Hugo

Some of the most talented CEOs whom I have worked with understand the power of inspiration. They know how to rally people around a shared vision of the future. They blend passion, energy, and enthusiasm into compelling messages that resonate with the masses. They are great storytellers and understand how to captivate and galvanize an audience. One of the most inspirational leaders I have worked with was Gary, a CEO of a midmarket pharmaceuticals company. I started working with Gary when he was a COO and was being groomed as a potential successor to the current CEO. The board wanted several of the internal CEO Succession candidates to work with executive coaches to refine their talents and leadership capabilities. After a series of chemistry meetings, Gary selected me as his coach, and we started our engagement together.

As Gary and I started our coaching relationship, I quickly realized the he was not your typical senior executive. Born and raised in central Florida, Gary was an active and athletic child. He played a variety of sports throughout childhood. From baseball to soccer to football, he began cultivating certain leadership skills at a very young age—skills like teamwork, influence, and partnering with others to accomplish a goal. He was also being exposed to different types of leadership styles with each of the coaches he worked with. Although these experiences helped shape his early ideas around leadership, it was the game of basketball that had a lasting impact on him in the early part of his life.

For Gary, basketball was tremendously inspiring. In one of our first coaching sessions, he talked about the impression Magic Johnson made on him as a teenager. This was during the mid '80s when the Los Angeles Lakers and Boston Celtics were exchanging NBA championships every year. Gary's father was a die-hard Lakers's fan, and he remembers the impact this had on him at an early age. Lakers games were always on during the spring in his parents' living room. Watching Magic Johnson did something to Gary. It inspired him to look at what it took to be a great leader. As we all know, Magic was the point guard for the Lakers, so he always had the ball in his hands before any other player would touch it. Unlike many of his contemporaries, Magic was a selfless floor general. He exceled when engaging and impacting his teammates. This was primarily accomplished through the assists he would have during games. He got the ball to others in such an innovative and creative manner. He inspired his teammates to compete and give all they could toward accomplishing their collective goals. This taught Gary the power of influence and how to inspire and motivate others. It also taught him the power of words and storytelling.

Gary began playing basketball in middle school and exceled at the sport in high school. He was given a scholarship to attend a prominent Division I school where he played point guard for his team. Emulating what he learned from Magic, Gary took a selfless approach to leadership. He placed teammates before himself. He was always encouraging and promoted the successes of others. He never took credit for his successes. It was always about the team and their collective goals. This inspired others to give their all. Teammates wanted to win for their coach and the university, but they also were committed to Gary. It was some of these early life lessons that began to shape the type of leader he wanted to be.

Gary started his career as a sales rep for a medical devices company. He had a region that covered parts of central and western Florida. He learned many things as a sales rep. He learned how to influence the thoughts and actions of others. How the power of words could cultivate trust or damage relationships. He learned about the importance of reciprocity. He learned how to be strategic but also detail-oriented in his approach to working with others. Within eighteen months, he was promoted to a district manager with responsibility for nine sales reps. This was his first management experience as a professional. Given his leadership role as a point guard for his college basketball team, he knew how to have a positive impact on others. He found that many of the lessons he learned from hoops translated into the workplace. In getting to know his team, he did four important things. First, he took time to connect with each person on the team. He took rides with them to their customers and invested in building a personal and professional relationship. He knew how to use his relational intelligence to form lasting bonds with his people. Second, he brought the team together on a regular basis to establish, and then reinforce, his vision. This gave the team a collective goal and a unified purpose. Third, he modeled the right behaviors for others. He never asked his sales reps to do something that he would not do. This garnered loyalty and commitment from the team. Lastly, he was always supportive and encouraging. He celebrated successes in public and provided development feedback in private conversations. These leadership behaviors served as a foundation for inspiring his team.

As Gary moved up in the organization from a district manager to a regional manager and then to a vice president of sales, he continued to focus on the skills and behaviors he implemented with his first team. After twelve years with the same organization, he was approached by a headhunter to join a pharmaceuticals biotech start-up. Gary joined his current employer as a vice president of sales and marketing. The new responsibilities for marketing gave him the opportunity to learn a new part of the business and how to expand his influence on a larger team. Within three years, the company had doubled its revenues, and Gary was promoted to a president and general manager for an entire division of the company. Although he had immense responsibility as a GM, he continued to take time for people and invest in relationships. This was a hallmark of his leadership. Over the next six years, Gary learned how to manage an entire P&L, helped R&D launch several new products, and played an active role in supporting HR with many critical hires. He became known for the inspirational speeches he delivered every year at the company's national sales meeting. He was great at rallying the troops and giving people a purpose and mission. People knew Gary served a higher purpose. This was not just about making money for the company. It was about how their drugs saved lives. Gary also led the philanthropic part of the business. He was regularly leading events for the local community and was a spokesperson for the company to the market and external stakeholders.

Shortly after the company went public, Gary was promoted to COO. The primary goal of our coaching work was to help prepare him as a possible successor to the founder and CEO. Our coaching work focused on three areas: getting Gary more access and visibility to investors and Wall Street, cultivating stronger relationships with the Board, and helping him grow the international business. Again, Gary leveraged experiences from earlier in his career to achieve his goals. He spent time with the CEO on road shows to interact with investors. He took time to build personal relationships with each of the board members. He built a new leadership team to drive the company's expansion outside of the US. He let me sit in on his first meeting with his leadership team, and his actions blew my mind. He spoke with great passion and enthusiasm about the company's vision for the future. He laid out a concrete plan for how expansion would take place. He spoke at length about the company's mission to save lives and how important it was to him personally. I watched how he captivated his audience and empowered them to accomplish their goals.

Over the next two years, Gary's leadership continued to shine. He had cultivated strong relationships with investors and the board. The company was successful in expanding across Europe and into Asia. Given these accomplishments and the financial success the company had during that time frame, he was promoted to CEO. We continued to work together as the board and CEO outlined their transition. What inspired me the most was how he handled the relationship with his predecessor. He understood that the company was the founder's baby. He ensured the current CEO understood his vision for the future. Gary committed to keeping lines of communication open after the transition. Gary was an inspirational leader. People gravitated to him throughout his career. His commitment to others, the investments he made in relationships, and his passion for the business had a positive impact on all the people he interacted with.

Why Inspiration Matters

Inspiration is about motivating, encouraging, and influencing others. Inspirational leaders empower others to make their highest and best contributions. They model a positive attitude and set the right example for others. They lead by their actions rather than words. They earn people's trust by delivering on promises and sticking to their commitments. They employ various influence strategies to meet the needs of different stakeholders. They collaborate and encourage collaboration across the organization. They relate to a vast array of people by understanding and appreciating diversity. They are authentic and genuine. They possess sufficient humility and appropriately compromise with others to achieve goals and objectives.

I have found that inspiration is a skill most leaders are born with. However, the ability to mold this skill into what they want must be learned and attentively cultivated. Some of my most inspirational clients credit their ability to influence others from working with other inspirational leaders. Ashley, a senior vice president of HR, developed the skill to have a positive and lasting impact on others early in her life. She was an avid learner and looked for role models that were both inspirational and charismatic before she started her career. During her college years, she gravitated toward professors who were not only teachers but encouraged the hopes and dreams of their students. This sparked an early desire to identify how to motivate others. She further explored this skill by getting involved in several student organizations and learning from other leaders of these groups. She learned about the power of words and how to captivate an audience. She learned how to recognize and reward the behaviors and actions of others. She learned how to mentor and support people. By the time she started her career, she had developed the capabilities to influence and inspire the work of others.

We started our work together after her company acquired a smaller organization. Ashley was tasked with developing a leadership competency framework that integrated the values and beliefs of the two organizations. Competency models are interesting things. When designed and implemented correctly, they can serve as unifying and galvanizing force for employees. When developed too quickly, or without enough buy-in and support, they tend to find their place on a shelf. Ashley didn't want their competency model to be created in vain. We talked through how to make it have the most meaningful impact on employees across the organization. We knew that we had to find key stakeholders from both companies that were passionate about leadership—those who were committed to the successful merger of two distinct cultures. We outlined a process that involved interviewing a number of senior leaders from both organizations. We conducted focus groups with midlevel management and launched an engagement and culture survey with employees at lower levels of the business. This allowed everyone to have a voice, to feel like they were contributing to the new leadership framework.

As we began to analyze and aggregate the findings, it became apparent that one culture valued collaboration while the other placed a strong emphasis on execution. One company liked to make decisions by committee while the other company operated with decision power resting on those who were in the highest positions of leadership. We also found that one company valued innovation while the other tended to value history and tradition. The task ahead of us was daunting. How would we get two distinct cultures to align and agree on shared leadership competencies? Ashley was quick to share the results with her CHRO. We then met with her CEO to discuss his strategic vision for the company's next stage of growth.

What I started to notice about Ashley is that she brought people together consistently to engage and get their points of view. This created a culture of partnership and made colleagues feel that their thoughts mattered. Over the next six months, she influenced the way people looked at the company. She had the ability to impact people without having the authority to do so. She empowered others to play a role in shaping the new work environment. She moved people emotionally by her steadfast passion and commitment to the new culture. It was her words that had a lasting impact. People believed what she had to say. It helped change behavior, get others aligned, and charted the course for their future.

Words Have Power

I've always been fascinated by sports. Golf is my first passion. I play the sport regularly, but am also an avid fan. Whether it's Tiger, Brooks Koepka, Justin Thomas, or Rory McIlroy, golfers' focus, commitment, grit, and determination are inspiring to watch. My second favorite sport is football. Not for the game itself, although NFL games can be some of the most exciting sporting events to watch. It is for the power that coaches have to motivate and inspire their players. One of my favorite coaches is Tony Dungy. I started following him in the late '90s when he was the coach of the Tampa Bay Buccaneers. Now football coaches can be interesting characters. Some have fiery, intense personalities. They know how to use words to build up or crush their players' spirits. Coaches like Tom Coughlin and Bill Belichick come to mind when I think of those types of leaders. Tony, on the other hand, was unique in his leadership style. He understood the power of words.

In his book *Quiet Strength*, he talks about how words can chart the course of a team's destiny. He discusses how coaches are responsible for everything they say. Their words send powerful messages to players and staff. He believed that what he said as a coach defined who he was as a leader. I never saw Tony chastise or put down his players. He encouraged and supported them. He used words to empower and promote the success of others. He let his values and beliefs as person, and as a leader, come through in the ways that he worked with others. I saw his style have a tremendous impact on his players. It helped shape the leadership styles of players like Peyton Manning, Marvin Harrison, Edgerrin James, and Jeff Saturday. When he was the coach of the Indianapolis Colts, his unique philosophy and leadership style helped propel the team to seven straight playoff appearances and a win in Super Bowl XLI. It was his use of words that helped get his team to the top of the NFL.

In my coaching work, I've seen leaders who have used words to inspire and build people up, and I've seen leaders who are destructive in how they engage and interact with others. This is especially the case with written communications and e-mail. Some of the most damaging things failed leaders do is communicate down to their employees. I've seen leaders disrespect and put people down over e-mail. I've seen them instill fear and apprehension with their people. They will argue that tough leadership is what is needed to drive results. This is anything further from the truth. Our words are a witness to who we are as people. Leaders should always model the right behaviors through what they say. Good leaders are careful not to speak rashly, impulsively, and out of anger. They take time to reflect on how they will interact with their people and teams in good times and in bad.

I encourage all my clients to speak with measured words. Words of encouragement and support can have a tremendous positive effect on the people around them. When employees feel valued and appreciated, it inspires commitment and loyalty to the organization. It promotes creative thinking and innovation. It helps people maximize their potential and achieve their desired outcomes. I've worked with many CEOs who understand the power of words.

Michael, a CEO in the telecommunications industry, was an expert at communication. I started working with his leadership team when they were looking to hire a new CIO. I found out right away how he used words to build people up. In our first meeting, he was quick to compliment me and the work of our firm. He was referred to us by a colleague I worked with many years ago. Michael didn't have to make an effort to establish that connection. I was trying to get him as a client! With time, I continued to see that this was a stable of his leadership. I saw this with his direct reports. I saw it with the candidates he had us assess. I saw it with the broader organization. He inspired people through his words and his actions. He moved people emotionally when he was in front of an audience. He was always honest, transparent, and clear in all his interactions with others.

Words are essential to any inspirational leader. Trust is earned by how leaders communicate with others. What they say and how they say it matters. When leaders model the right attitude and set a positive example for how people are to engage and communicate with one another, it is contagious to an organization. Their words can bring people together from diverse background and drive buy-in, alignment, and commitment to goals and objectives.

Carrots and Sticks: Rewards, Recognition, and Repercussions

Inspiration is about more than just words. It is how leaders recognize and reward the contributions of their people. Inspirational leaders use the right incentives to motivate desired behaviors from others. Rewards are more than just salary raises and bonuses. These things are no doubt important, but they are prices of admission when it comes to acknowledging the work of others. Leaders who reward others through multiple means (e.g., vacations, extended time off, work from home privileges, gift cards, access to training and development opportunities) tend to get the best out of their teams. They know how to promote high performance by offering desired outcomes that are valuable to employees.

Using positive reinforcement is one of the best ways to reward people. The psychologist B. F. Skinner was one of the first to study the effects of positive reinforcement on behavior. His operant conditioning model is based on the assumption that studying a behavior's cause and its consequences is the best way to understand and regulate it. His work expanded on the work of Edward Thorndike's "law of effect," which stated that a behavior that is followed by pleasant or desirable outcome is likely to be repeated. Skinner defined positive reinforcement as introducing a desired stimulus to encourage the desired behavior. In his work, he outlined four types of positive reinforcement: (a) natural reinforcers—reinforcers that occur directly as a result of the desired behavior (e.g., if a sales rep hits a targeted revenue number, they receive a specific bonus amount); (b) token reinforcers—those who are awarded for performing certain behaviors and can be exchanged for something of value (e.g., if an employee receives a positive customer satisfaction review, they can be awarded an added vacation day or a $500 Amazon gift card); (c) social reinforcers—those who involve a leader expressing their approval of a behavior (e.g., if an employee does great work, a leader saying, "Great job!" or "Excellent work" at a staff meeting); and (d) tangible forcers—reinforces that are actual physical or tangible rewards (e.g., if an employee exceeds performance expectations, they receive and new iPad or iPhone). As you might expect, the effectiveness of a reinforcer depends on the context. In a medical devices or pharmaceutical company, natural reinforcers are highly valued. In a retail company, tangible reinforcers are typically attractive to employees.

Although there are other types of rewards that are effective in the right contexts, there are unique benefits to positive reinforcement. First, research has shown that positive reinforcement is effective in the long-term. Employees have a clear understanding of what is rewarded and the types of rewards that exist for high performance. Second, a positive reinforcement plan allows leaders to encourage productive work behaviors. In Skinner's research, he devised five different approaches to encouraging new behaviors: (a) continuous reinforcement—the behavior is reinforced after each and every behavior occurs; (b) fixed-ration reinforcement—the behavior is reinforced after a specific number of occurrences (e.g., after every five times a behavior is performed); (c) fixed-interval reinforcement—the behavior is reinforced after a specific amount of time (e.g., a week or a month); (d) variable-ratio reinforcement—the behavior is reinforced after a variable number of occurrences (e.g., after four occurrences, then after another two, then after another eight); and (e) variable-interval reinforcement—the behavior is reinforced after a variable amount of time (e.g., after ten days, then after three and then after nine).

In organizational contexts, the two best reinforcement schedules are the fixed-ratio and fixed-interval schedules. For example, with the fixed-ratio, a sales rep is given an incentive after ten new sales. With the fixed-interval, a high-performing employee is given a reward at the end of the month or quarter. Regardless, of the type of reinforcement or its schedule, employees work best when they are rewarded and recognized for their efforts. Leaders who understand this get the best out of their people. They can also use the reward incentives to motivate and drive performance. The truly inspirational leaders do this in a way that promotes teamwork and collaboration. Internal competition is good but can have negative long-term ramifications. Employees are usually highly motivated when their leader is fair in how they distribute rewards and recognition.

Although rewards and recognition are critical to success, leaders must also hold people accountable. There should always be repercussions if goals—performance or developmental—are not attained. The inspirational leader knows how to set clear expectations and hold people accountable to results. We touched on accountability in our chapter on vigilance, but it is important to reiterate it here. Inspiration leaders are excellent at following up to ensure progress is being made against desired outcomes. They will give people freedom and autonomy but are there as a resource when needed. They are encouraging and supportive but are consistent in providing oversight and direction.

Harry, a senior vice president of a food and beverage company, was great at getting people to deliver results and exceed performance expectations. I was brought in to help one of his team members who had been underperforming for several months. There were reports that this leader was being too harsh with his team and that he needed to change his influence style. Harry played an active role in the coaching engagement from the start. He was open and transparent with his concerns and what repercussions would take place if his direct report didn't work on changing his approach. Although his direct report understood the changes that needed to take place, he was combative and difficult to work with. He felt the organization was doing him a disservice and humiliating him by subjecting him to working with an executive coach. Harry did his best to reassure his leader that this was not the case. He played an active role in supporting his direct report the best that he could.

We had monthly touch points to make sure progress was being made against the personal development plan. He didn't have to do this. Harry could have let his leader figure things out on his own. Inspirational leaders don't do that though. They want to see all their people succeed and will do what they can to ensure that takes place.

After several months, his direct report started to make a change. Our biggest breakthrough was at a midway alignment meeting. Harry listened to what his direct report had done to make changes to his leadership style. He reinforced how critical this individual was to the team. He told him where he was still missing the mark but reaffirmed his commitment to his success. I walked out of the meeting feeling positive about our next steps. So did his direct report. Within six months, we started to see dramatic changes in his leadership. When we met for our wrap-up alignment session, his direct report credited the changes to the support that Harry provided. He finally understood that people weren't out to get him. It was about the team, his people, and striving to be their best. Harry did this with all his people. He was clear on expectations, challenged people to be their best, and held them accountable if that didn't take place. Inspirational leaders understand what buttons to push. They do so in an encouraging and supportive manner, but it is their commitment to people that ignites passion and allows their team members to reach their goals.

Developing People

Inspirational leaders are talent developers. They understand that the greatest asset to any organization is their people. Over the course of my career, I've seen many different approaches to developing people. Some leaders take a one-on-one approach. They take time for each team member and align their personal goals and objectives to that of the team. They help people figure out what their strengths and opportunities are and find ways to help people unleash their potential. Other leaders take a team-oriented approach. They bring their people together to work on ways to be a collaborative and cohesive team. These leaders are great at setting vision and expectations and then letting people have the autonomy to perform at their high levels.

I've always been a strong supporter of high-potential leadership development programs. These programs typically have a combination of methods and approaches to strengthen talent. I also believe these programs help people grow the fastest. The truly inspirational leaders understand this because they know people grow best when there is a combination of self-exploration, feedback, training, and action learning. Christine, a retail executive whom I worked with several years ago, was a strong people developer. We started working together when her organization was going through their annual talent review. Every year, her company reviewed their talent to determine which leaders were ready to take on greater scale, scope, and responsibility. One of the outcomes of the talent reviews was to accelerate the growth of their next generation leaders. She had some strong successors in key roles but wanted to strengthen the bench. To do this, we outlined a six-month high-potential development program.

Any successful high potential leadership development program has five critical components. Once leaders have been identified for the program, they first need to be assessed. Assessment can include many different components. A strong assessment process will typically involve some type of personality test. In our firm, we use the Hogan leadership forecast assessment. It's a great tool to get at a leader's strengths, derailers, and their values/beliefs. We will then conduct a 360-degree assessment. This can be accomplished through interviews or by using an online tool. The last part, and this is the most critical, is a behavioral interview. The assessment interview allows leaders to explore how their experiences have shaped who they are as people and as leaders. Once we have data from all these sources, a leader is given a feedback report to help them understand their leadership strengths and areas of opportunity. Feedback sets the stage for the rest of the program because it gives a leader the starting point through which they can grow.

The second component of a strong high-potential program is development planning. With development planning, leaders get the chance to outline two or three goals they want to accomplish over the course of the program. I will usually have them share the plan with their manager in a three-way alignment meeting to ensure all stakeholders are on the same page with respect to the leader's goals and objectives. Third, there is usually an executive education training component that is added to the program. This enables leaders to learn new skills and capabilities over the course of the six-month program. In Christine's case, we identified four topics—emotional intelligence, innovation and creativity, conflict management, and enterprise leadership—that we would build a curriculum around. We brought the group together once a month for a two-day offsite to go through the content of each topic.

Fourth, a strong talent program involves coaching or mentoring. Coaching is helpful because it gives leaders a chance to work through their development plans while incorporating what they are learning at each of the training off-sites. It is a safe environment where leaders can engage with a trusted thought partner on their progress and growth. Mentoring is helpful because it allows a leader to be exposed to more senior-level executives who can help them understand the broader landscape in the organization. It is also an avenue for transfer of wisdom and experience. Christine opted to go forward with mentoring, and we identified a mentor for each leader in the program. If you're going to use the mentoring model, it is good to have a cohort of twelve to fifteen people in the program so that a mentor can be use with each leader. Having a group larger than fifteen can be too demanding on the organization given the amount of time that is needed for the mentoring partnerships.

The final component of a strong high-potential program is action learning. Action-learning projects give leaders an opportunity to work together as a team to solve a challenge facing the organization. Action-learning projects can range from developing a new product or service offering to looking for new ways to impact clients or customers. In Christine's case, we put together two action-learning projects. Half of the group got to work on designing a new conceptual framework for how their retail stores would look in the future. The other half got to work on developing ways to enhance the customer experience in their stores. Action learning is a great vehicle for understanding team dynamics. Who takes on the leadership role for the team? Who makes sure the team is accountable for achieving the desired outcomes? Who are the people who quickly begin to execute on the priorities? Who focuses on relationships and making sure the team works together cohesively? All these questions are explored in an action-learning project. As an organizational psychologist, it is fascinating to me to see how the team dynamic begins to take shape. Each leader has their own personal development goals, and the action-learning projects give them a chance in a safe environment to work on their individual objectives.

The high-potential program we put together for Christine's organization was a huge success. All of their leaders came out of the program with (a) a greater understanding of their individual capabilities, (b) exposure to senior leaders and opportunities to learn and grow from them, and (c) ways to partner with others to form a team and accomplish an important organizational objective. The high-potential program became a stable for Christine's organization. Graduates of the program were promoted faster than those who did not participate in the program. What was most exciting to me was that the mentoring relationships that were established tended to extend beyond duration of the program. Mentoring became part of the company's culture.

Inspirational leaders focus on the growth and development of their people. Whether it is individually, collectively, or through a talent development program, leaders who treat people as the company's number one asset get the most out of their employees. As a firm that prides ourselves on helping people maximize their full potential, I am always pleased to see when leaders invest in supporting the growth of their people. Companies that do this create cultures of excellence. They also unlock opportunities for innovation and creativity. The topic we will explore in depth in our next chapter.

Action Steps for Leading with Inspiration

Consistently reinforce the vision

Inspirational leaders know how to set a vision for others to follow. If you want to motivate people and drive commitment, you need to be able to captivate your audience around a shared mission and purpose. So how do you consistently reinforce your organization's vision? There are several critical steps. First, you need to create alignment and agreement. Your employees need to feel that they have skin in the game. They need to feel that the work they do contributes to the bigger picture. They have to see how the work that is done in the short-term will have a lasting impact in the long run. Some of the greatest leaders I have worked with know how to inspire in both good in bad times.

Last year, in my work with Mark, a telecommunications CEO, we mapped out how his organization would respond to the COVID-19 crisis. The pandemic impacted organizations across all industries. It was a challenging and difficult times for our entire nation. His call to action was to unite his people around the organization's mission. In his first e-mail to all the leaders of the company, he outlined why compassion and empathy were needed more than ever. He encouraged his people to keep open lines of communication with their people and with their customers. He spoke about the need for constant information sharing so that people would know the actions the company was taking in response to the crisis. He emphasized the importance of stability and how his leaders needed to model steadfast commitment to the company's leadership principles. What was truly inspirational was how he tied each leadership principle to ways his people needed to lead in times of uncertainty. For example, one of their leadership competencies is championing teamwork. He outlined that the response to the crisis presented a unique opportunity for leaders to take teamwork to a level never achieved before. The company's employees would not be able to drive results unless his leaders took time to establish new teamwork processes that would last long after the crisis ended. I saw people rally behind his vision. They took responsibility for the actions of their teams and how they would better serve their customers. His steady leadership during the crisis is a testament to who Mark is as an inspirational CEO.

Moving beyond creating alignment, inspirational leaders make course corrections to the vision as circumstances change. If you are going to inspire people, you need to be flexible and adaptable. You need to be able to adjust your sails as the currents shift. This is where some leaders get into trouble. They can develop tunnel vision and lose sight of how people are responding to the vision. If business changes occur (e.g., economic factors, customer trends, competition), the inspirational leader needs to reevaluate the course they have set and make the necessary adjustments. Lastly, inspirational leaders live the vision and mission. They model the right behaviors for others, which engenders loyalty and commitment to excellence. Leaders who walk the talk show employees that they are willing to make the necessary sacrifices to succeed. Without this, people can become disengaged and lose sight of their goals and priorities.

So, remember, inspirational leaders are consistent with their vision. Make sure you are clear with where you want others to follow. Get their input and encourage them to play an active role in charting the course. Be flexible. Listen to your people when they have questions or concerns. Be willing to make real-time adjustments as new data and information presents itself. The leaders who can adapt are the ones who tend to thrive. Above all else, reinforce the vision by living it out in your daily behaviors and actions. Your people are looking up to you for guidance and direction. They want to feel secure in knowing what they do is linked to what you do. They want their efforts to reflect the strategic priorities for the business. And they want to know that their personal values and beliefs are linked to the core mission of the organization.

Speak words of encouragement

As a leader, what you say matters. People look up to you. They want your encouragement and support. When you recognize and praise people, it goes a long way. I encourage my clients to choose their words wisely. The right comment at the right time reinforces the value employees bring to the team. It can motivate them to continue to exceed expectations and deliver results.

There are three approaches to speaking words of encouragement. First, there are the random comments throughout a day or work week. For example, if one of your employees gets a sale or someone achieves a goal, a simple comment like "Great job," "This work is really impressive," or "I appreciate what you do," can brighten a person's day. It makes people feel good about themselves. Make sure you spread the support around your whole team. Don't leave people out. Everyone contributes in some fashion. Find ways to encourage them, and do it consistently.

Second, it is great to praise people in front of others. Team meetings are an excellent venue for this. Make sure you do your homework and put your thoughts together beforehand. Be specific. People can tell when a comment isn't genuine or sincere. Several years back, I worked with James, a senior vice president of sales for a consumer products company. He was great at supporting and championing his people in front of others. He would regularly promote the accomplishments of his direct reports in front of peers or senior management. It was nothing spectacular. Just consistent praise and recognition for the work they did. I was brought in to work with his team to help them get aligned on new goals for the upcoming year. In my one-on-one sessions with each of his leaders, they all spoke at length about how much support he provided to them. They were most grateful for how he recognized them in front of others. This made his people work harder but also work collaboratively as they thrived off the positive feedback.

Third, it is great to provide words of encouragement during regular one-on-one meetings. You can go into more details in these settings and talk about your people's work at length. This is where coaching and feedback becomes so critical. Unfortunately, many leaders miss the mark with feedback. They become so fixated on results and the numbers that they forget to provide coaching and support. When I work with leaders who need to be more focused on their people, I will start by having them take me through their team members and identifying what they do well and what they struggle with. We discuss what each direct report brings to their team, but I also encourage the leader to make a consistent habit of taking time for developmental conversations.

Your people want that time with you. They want you to focus on how they can grow and improve. They want to become better leaders. So find time to have regular one-on-one meetings with all your people. Spend the time that you need to on the business, but carve out a portion of the meeting to talk about their goals and interests. Focus on things that are important to their professional development. Let them know that you value what they do, that you're there to support them, and that you're committed to their success. It will go a long way with your people, and they will work harder for you and for the organization.

Make a commitment to excellence by selecting the best talent

People look to their leaders for inspiration. They want to be led by someone who is passionate and aspires to a higher calling. Employees aren't looking for leaders who are perfect, though. Excellence is what matters most. Do you go above and beyond to achieve your goals and objectives? Are you promoting teamwork and collaboration? Are you humble, or do you put yourself before others? Do you need to have all the spotlight, or do you let your people have opportunities to shine? You have to be comfortable in your own skin and know who you are as a leader. Get your mission and purpose clear, and then unleash others to do the work.

Building a culture of excellence takes time. It starts with selecting and hiring great talent. In my work with organizations, talent selection is one of the most critical things that a company can do. Getting the right people in the door makes all the difference. So how do you find people who fit the bill? It starts with cultivating an understanding of where you want to take the business. Where do you see the company growing three to five years from now? Get clear about that. Then you have to determine the roles that will need to be filled to make your vision a reality. Do you need people who are strategic? Those who know how to execute? People who work together effectively as a team? Those who are innovative and creative? Those who have a growth mindset? The answer is yes to all of these questions. You also need to have diversity of thought and experience.

Once you have the framework in place, you need to invest in getting the selection process right. Rodney, a CEO in the hospitality industry, understood the importance of selecting the right people. He came to my firm with a simple request, "Help us hire the best people." We partnered with his company to create an assessment process that would get them the right talent for where they wanted to take the company. We use a rigorous selection assessment process at our firm. Our process begins with getting alignment on what the critical role imperatives and key leadership competencies are for specific roles within an organization. In Rodney's case, we were helping his company assess for several critical roles. We helped them determine what the unique role imperatives were for each role and then put together a set of leadership competencies that represented the company's values and culture. Our assessment scorecards, as we call them, help us to get laser focused on what it will take to be successful in the organization.

Once a scorecard has been established, most companies work with executive recruiters to get a slate of candidates whom they are interested in pursuing. We always encourage our clients to do one or two rounds of exploratory conversations to see if there is a potential fit. These conversations give candidates a feel for the company, and they allow key stakeholders to determine whom they want to move forward with in the process. These conversations also surface specific questions or concerns that the company may have about particular candidates. These questions are usually shared with us so that we can dive deeper into the topics during our assessment interviews. Rodney had several important questions about two of their candidates. He wanted to know if one of the individuals would mesh well with the personalities on his executive leadership team. For the other, he was concerned about their leadership style and if it would fit well with the company's values and beliefs.

When we assess leaders, we are always looking for a number of variables that will make a good fit. We explore the candidate's work history to get the critical role imperatives. We talk through their leadership experiences to get at the company's leadership principles. We also assess for potential and a candidate's ability to work well with others. Often, given what we know about the company and its senior leaders, we can determine if an individual's personality and values will mesh well with others. With the two leaders we assessed for Rodney, several things surfaced that were red flags. The first leader had a domineering and aggressive communication style. They usually had to be the loudest voice in a room and were combative when people disagreed with them. I witnessed this firsthand during our interview when the candidate snapped back at several of our questions! The second candidate had a laissez-faire leadership style and was very hands-off with their people. The candidate didn't have the level of passion and drive that Rodney and many of his leaders possessed. In the end, we did not recommend either candidate, and it saved their organization valuable time and money that would have been wasted when the leaders started to derail and struggle acclimating to the culture. We eventually helped them select the right talent, and it helped to strengthen their organization and promote the type of excellence that Rodney expected of his senior executives.

I cannot stress the importance of getting the right leaders in the right roles when you're attempting to build a culture of excellence. When you have the right people, it is easy to get them focused and aligned on what matters most. You then need to encourage them to champion and promote the company's strategic vision with their teams and people. Their focus on excellence has to reflect the things you do and say as a leader. When you do this, you'll see mountains move. Excellence starts with you. As a leader, it is what you do and say on a consistent business that leaves a lasting impression with others.

INNOVATION

The only way to discover the limits of the possible
is to go beyond them into the impossible.
—Arthur C. Clarke

Alex understood the power of innovation. From an early age, he was a curious and inquisitive child. As the youngest of three, he was exposed to a variety of hobbies and activities from his siblings. He enjoyed playing sports, gravitating toward soccer and long-distance running. He did well in school, regularly bringing home straight A's on his report cards. He had a diverse group of friends. This exposed him to a variety of people with different backgrounds, values, and beliefs. It wasn't until middle school, though, that he found his true passion in music. Alex started to play the violin and became an exceptionally skilled musician. With music, he was able to tap into his innovative side and express himself creatively. Throughout high school, Alex continued to play the violin and got to perform in orchestras at the state and regional level. He also continued to excel in his studies and was accepted to a prestige university to study business.

In college, Alex continued to be involved in many different activities and social groups. He joined several student honor societies in his business school and took on a leadership role running the student radio station. It was during these years that he started to cultivate certain skills as a leader. He learned about the importance of teamwork. He learned how to build relationships quickly with people from different background and ethnicities. Alex started his career in financial services where he was exposed to operations and technology, two areas that would play a role throughout his career. Within seven years, he had worked his way up to a vice president position where he oversaw teams in one of the highest-revenue-generating business units in the company. Alex became known as a strategic problem solver. Over the next ten years, he was involved in leading several organizational restructures and developed a reputation for driving transformation. He also cultivated the skills to effectively lead large teams. Many of the members of his team were promoted to significant roles in the company. This was a testament to his ability to develop talent.

After twenty-five years with one company and many promotions up through the ranks, Alex wanted to take on a new challenge. He was approached by a headhunter to take on an executive leadership role in an insurance company. Although he had little experience in insurance, he welcomed the opportunity to take on a new challenge. He joined the firm as the chief operating officer and had responsibility over corporate strategy, technology, operations, branding and communication, strategic sourcing, and customer solutions. His CEO gave him a mandate to focus on three areas. First, he was to lead a full enterprise transformation for the firm. Second, his teams were responsible for onboarding new businesses into the organization and making sure that operations were able to integrate the new businesses successfully. Lastly, he was to improve the firm's branding and communications strategy.

Upon stepping into the role, Alex spent the first six months getting to know his people and teams, and the culture of the organization. He made several changes to his leadership team and brought in strong talent to support the key initiatives he was responsible for leading. Once he assembled the right talent on his leadership team, he brought the group together to outline his vision for the future. He solicited input and counsel from his direct reports and the team aligned on key strategic priorities. He also established three cultural pillars for how his organization was to operate moving forward. The pillars focused on developing their people, innovating with big ideas, and striving for excellence.

Alex first went to work on the technology organization. His teams did an upgrade to their entire IT organization, they brought in third-party vendors to support the onboarding of the new businesses, and they created a joint-venture partnership with a group that would take on most of the day-to-day technology and IT responsibilities. Within eighteen months, technology had completed a significant number of large strategic initiatives while improving security and operational risk, and lowering their operating costs. His teams continued to excel on delivering against their goals and objectives. As Alex continued to make changes in the organization, he started to get strong resistance and pushback from his three largest internal customers. The leaders of the three key business units in the firm began complaining that he was driving too much change without getting their buy-in and approval. This caused friction between his teams and leaders in the business units.

After six months of challenges, I was asked to come in and coach Alex. His CEO wanted us to work on two areas. First, he wanted Alex to cultivate stronger relationships with his peers on the executive leadership team. Second, he wanted Alex and his teams to get more exposure to the business. He felt that if Alex got out into the business more, he would have a better understanding of how to support his internal customers. In my first session with Alex, we talked about his leadership style, his impressions of the organization, and his point of view as to how the challenges with his peers developed over time. Alex believed that he was given the mandate to innovate and drive change for the firm, but that his peers were accustomed to tradition and the status quo. They did not want to evolve and accept the changes that were needed. This caused most of the issues between his organization and the business units. This is a classic issue that I see with many of my clients. A leader is asked to join the organization and drive change, but many of their colleagues want things to stay the same. To dive deeper into the issues, I recommended that we conduct a 360-degree assessment to determine what themes were emerging across the organization about his leadership. Alex thought this was a great idea as he had now been with the company for two years and had received little feedback from others. We put a 360-participant list together that included his direct reports, peers, external business partners, and senior leadership. We ran the list by the

CHRO for his alignment with the participants, and I began conducting my interviews.

As I analyzed all the interview data, three themes emerged. First, Alex's people loved working for him. They saw him as a breath of fresh air that was bringing about the changes the organization needed to thrive in the future. They also found him to be a strong leader. Alex got the team focused on the vision, gave them the freedom and autonomy to perform their job responsibilities, and provided his support whenever they needed it. Second, his peers, most of whom had long tenures with the organization, wanted full power to run their businesses. They believed it was their responsibility to oversee all aspects of their operations and technology teams. The corporate functions needed to deliver what they wanted and give them full authority to make the decisions that would improve how they ran their businesses. They also saw little value in making changes. Things had worked fine for many years, and they were comfortable with the status quo. Lastly, his CEO had a laid-back and laissez-faire leadership style. He rarely stepped in to address conflicts with his direct reports, which gave the business unit leaders freedom to challenge most of the programs that Alex wanted to implement for the firm. This was a perfect storm. Alex had teams that wanted to innovate and drive change, but he had peers who didn't think they needed the changes and a CEO who didn't step in to support his efforts. When I shared the feedback with Alex, he wasn't surprised.

Now Alex was a confident and courageous senior executive. He had little problem challenging the perspectives of others and fought for what he believed would strengthen the way the firm operated. We had to change the perception that he did what he felt the company needed without getting the buy-in and support from his peers. So we focused on two developmental goals for our coaching. First, he needed to strengthen his relationships with all his peers. Second, he needed to get out into the business and learn what the teams needed from his organization to be successful.

What I admired about Alex is that he took the feedback to heart and worked on what he felt he needed to do to drive greater alignment with his colleagues. Over the next year, Alex strengthened his partnerships with his peers. He listened more and spoke less. He went out of his way to ensure the three business unit leaders were aligned with the changes his organization needed to make. He got out into the business and learned how his teams could better support the work of their colleagues. He cultivated greater relational intelligence. This changed the perception that he only cared about driving change and leading the enterprise transformation efforts. It made him come across as more engaging and collaborative.

In the end, Alex and his teams were able to deliver on all the key strategic initiatives for the organization. The enterprise transformation was completed ahead of schedule. The firm had successfully onboarded and integrated important new businesses. Their branding and communication efforts continued to increase while the firm spent less. Through the use of innovative social media and data analytics solutions, the firm was well positioned to thrive in the future. Alex's ability to apply continuous improvement and innovations to processes and procedures across the firm impacted the business at all levels. His ability to see problems from multiple angles, effectively manage complexity, and take calculated risks have made him successful for the organization. The combination of these skills will continue to have a positive impact on his leadership today and position him for greater responsibility in the future.

Anticipate the Future

Innovative leaders anticipate the unexpected and think with an eye toward the future. They are able to refine goals and objectives along the way. They are creative in how they address problems facing the business. They prioritize and focus people on the most critical levers that will drive success. When a leader is innovative, they are able to see around corners and can balance near-term objectives with long-term goals. They also reward and celebrate the innovations of others. They encourage people to think about problems differently and "think outside the box." They aren't reckless risk-takers. They are strong problems solvers and critical thinkers that take calculated risks to grow the business. They probe deeply to understand root cause of issues in order to create viable plans for change.

Henry, a regional vice president for a retail company I worked with a few years back, understood how to drive innovation. He was a creative problem solver but, more importantly, knew how to unleash the innovative powers of his team. I had been coaching Henry for several months when we started to discuss the next evolution of growth for the company's stores. He thought the landscape was beginning to shift and customers wanted more than just a shopping experience. They wanted to connect with the products and have an experience when they visited the company's stores. So we began brainstorming ideas. What would create a more personal experience for their customers? What could their employees do that would foster that environment? Henry quickly put together a think tank with several of his direct reports. He gave them one simple mandate: come up with ideas that would enhance the customer's experience.

The think tank had a diverse group of leaders. There were people from different regions throughout his territory. He had a mix of men and women on the team. There were employees from different backgrounds and ethnicities. This fostered diversity of thought. It enabled the team to leverage alternative perspectives to deliver creative ideas that would help change the shopping experience. What I admired most about Henry was that he believed there was no bad idea. He encouraged people to think big. He wanted his people to challenge one another in their thinking. He created a safe environment where people could come up with ideas and take risks.

The team outlined three strategies, which varied depending on the region stores were located. For the New York Metropolitan area, the team came up with the idea to set up small stages and invite local bands to perform at certain hours of the day. They wanted to create music events that would drive greater traffic in their stores. There were a lot of logistics that needed to be managed, but Henry encouraged the team to move forward with the idea. He was continuously looking for them to innovate. For example, what stores saw the most traffic at certain times of the day? Where were the stores located in the city? What was the demographic of the customers that visited different stores? They learned lessons along the way, but Henry never shot down any of the team's ideas. They ran some pilot musical performances to gauge how customers would react. They took customer feedback and made adjustments along the way. Henry was flexible and adaptable as they made changes.

For another region, the team came up with the idea for in store demos of their newest products. They created parts of the store where employees would showcase Apple and Samsung products and made the demos interactive for customers to experience. They trained employees to be experts in the different product categories. Again, Henry encouraged them to try different ideas. If something did not work, he told them to go back to the drawing table and come up with new solutions. This approach fostered a sense of confidence that his people could come up with the right ideas to drive results. Over the next year, the team came up with many different innovative approaches to driving greater traffic into their stores. Some ideas stuck, and some didn't work. In the end, the think tank had come up with several ideas that gained traction and helped transform the shopping experience for their customers. It was Henry's commitment to innovative that gave birth to all their creative ideas.

Being able to anticipate the future is also about managing the unexpected. Innovative leaders are capable of prioritizing issues, and they use solid judgment to make changes that will support the business. They're highly adaptable. This enables them to confront external environmental factors with confidence. They can balance urgency while maintaining stability. Innovative leaders are also attuned to the competition. They stay up to date on what their competitors are doing and share this information with others. They identify potential threats early on and propose defensive and offensive strategies as appropriate.

Leaders struggle with innovation when their teams are made up of people who all think alike. The psychological concept of groupthink is one of the greatest detriments to innovation. Groupthink occurs when teams have a strong desire for harmony and conformity, which results in irrational or dysfunctional decision-making outcomes. It is the need for cohesiveness that produces the tendency for team members to agree about things at all costs. This causes a team to minimize the exchange of ideas and engage in healthy conflict that can spring about change.

When groupthink occurs, team members avoid raising controversial issues or alternative solutions; and there is a loss of individual creativity, uniqueness, and independent thinking. The dysfunctional group dynamics of these types of teams produces a one-size-fits-all approach to problem-solving. I often see groupthink in action when there is a leader with a strong personality. They tend to like things done a certain way and do not encourage employees to think differently. People conform out of the fear that they will lose approval from their leader if their ideas do not match the leader's agenda. When I am brought in to help teams break these patterns, it is critical that the leader steps back to take stock of how the team operates. They need to understand how much influence they are exerting. They also need to figure out what team members are more domineering than others. When leaders figure this information out, they can make changes that will allow the team to be more innovative and creative. It gives team members the ability to think differently, which enables people to focus on issues impacting today and plan for the future.

Putting Thoughts into Action

Innovative leaders know how to put thoughts into action. They are not afraid to unleash their creative talents and capabilities. They possess clarity about where things are today and can think forward into the future. They do not let distractions get in the way. Innovative leaders are visionaries. They plan ahead. They anticipate the needs of customers and can see trends unfolding in the external environment. They proactively use creativity and take calculated risks to improve work processes and create sustainable results. They allow team members to safely learn through trial and error and to fail forward in a safe manner.

I've come to learn that innovation is not just about idea creation, but it is about how to translate ideas into plans and actions—plans that individuals, teams, and organizations can put into practice. Early on in my career, I did a lot of consulting and coaching work with leaders in the medical devices industry. Medical devices sales reps have a tough job. They are constantly looking to drive sales and attain financial performance targets. I've worked with sales leaders who operate in the traditional manner. They stick with what's tried, tested, and true. This can be effective, but I've learned that the most successful sales leaders know how to come up with new and different ways to reach their customers.

Todd, a vice president of sales, whom I worked with many years ago was an innovative leader. He paid his dues in the field and learned how to connect with his customers. At the time, there were standard approaches to driving sales. Reps were assigned a region and needed to build relationships with different hospitals, doctors' offices, and medical facilities. Todd was a quick study. He was skilled at building connections easily. This brought him early success in his career. Early on, he began trying different ways to reach his customers. He came up with ideas like holding events for doctors and physicians to demo products. He connected with nurses and administrators to learn about how different hospital settings operated. He was always looking for ways to improve the partnerships with his customers. Some ideas didn't work. Some stuck, though. He kept a journal of his different ideas and always devised plans to implement new ideas that he came up with.

As he progressed from a rep to a district manager, he encouraged his people to do the same. His reps came up with some great ideas, but they often had difficulty implementing them. Some ideas were too grandiose. Other ideas presented challenges with resource allocations. Each time a direct report came to him with an idea, he coached them to put the idea into a plan and execute upon it. He encouraged them to try different things. He highlighted and celebrated ideas that translated into positive results. His willingness to come up with ideas and then attempt to implement them promoted a culture of nimble thinking. His people began anticipating and responding to changes in their operating landscapes.

Once he was promoted to regional manager, Todd had developed a reputation for driving innovation and change. He started having regular brainstorm meetings with his direct report team to devise creative solutions to exceed performance expectations. His region was consistently in the top five regions of the company because of their approach to meeting the needs of their customers. I was impressed by the culture he created with his people. They made course corrections quickly if ideas did not work. They came together to share learnings and readjust their approach. This ultimately got him into a VP role. It was his ability to use his creativity, and translate ideas into actions, that enabled his team to execute effectively. It was also his commitment to encouraging the innovations of others that made his team so successful.

The innovative leaders can implement their ideas. Regardless of the industry, the innovators tend to thrive. This is especially true right now in our world where access to information is so readily available. In retail for example, customers have a litany of shopping options at their fingertips. Through the use of mobile devices and online shopping, they can compare prices and look for the best deals. They can study products and categories quickly and easily. The innovative retail leaders have responded to this by building omnichannel strategies that put them on the cutting edge of meeting their customers' needs.

Organizational improvements need to be taken with decisive action. Innovative leaders know how to do this with speed and efficiency. They are willing to take ideas, quickly identify key levers that will drive growth, and put in place the processes and procedures that will get them there. Putting thoughts into action can be risky. Innovative thinkers have good discernment, though. They are not afraid to try different things. If they fail, they regroup and refocus their efforts. They also aren't afraid to challenge the ideas of others. They do it in a collaborative and supportive manner, but they appreciate the value of looking at things in different ways. Their ability to apply intellectual curiosity toward creating realistic solutions to complex problems enables them to drive change.

Building Cultures that Support Creativity

Innovation doesn't just happen with individuals or teams. It happens at the organizational level. Innovative organizations champion change, advocate continual improvements, and reward innovative solutions. It takes time to build a culture of innovation. Companies need to have senior executives who value change. They promote it throughout all levels of the organization. They encourage creative problem solving and support employees that think toward the future. They use their imagination, and the imaginations of their people, to develop solutions to complex challenges facing the world.

I've been a student of organizational culture for most of my career. I am fascinated by how culture shapes employees' values and beliefs. Good cultures evolve over time. They are mission driven. They practice consistent behaviors day-in and day-out. They involve their teams. They are agile and adaptable. One of the leading experts in the area of organizational culture, Daniel Denison, has spent his entire professional life focused on advancing the field of organizational development. His work has made many important contributions to the understanding of organizational culture and its relationship to the success of organizations. His Denison Model of Organizational Culture is the basis for one of the industry's leading organizational culture assessment tools. Research by his team has shown a strong relationship between organizational culture and business performance metrics such as profitability growth, customer satisfaction, and innovation.

I was exposed to Denison Organizational Culture Survey early on in my career. One of my first clients was interested in developing a culture that was focused on growth and innovation. They had recently acquired a technology platform and needed to integrate and assimilate two different company cultures. When I met with the firm's CEO, the mandate was simple: figure out how to combine the best parts of both companies and help them develop one culture focused on growth. He believed that as a result of the acquisition their new technologies could change the landscape for the industry. I quickly introduced him to the Denison Culture Model and outlined how we would assess the current state of affairs.

The Denison Organizational Culture Survey focuses on four areas: mission, consistency, involvement, and adaptability.

The mission dimension explores three areas:

a) *Strategic direction and intent*, which focuses on survey questions like "There is a long-term purpose and direction for the company" and "There is a clear strategy for our future."

b) *Goals and objectives*, which focuses on survey questions like "There is widespread agreement on goals" and "The leadership team has clearly stated the objectives we are trying to achieve."

c) *Vision*, which focuses on survey questions like "We have a shared vision of what the organization will be like in the future" and "Our vision creates excitement and motivation for our employees."

The consistency dimension explores the following:

a) *Core values*, which focuses on survey questions like "There is a clear and consistent set of values that governs the way we do business" and "There is an ethical code that guides our behavior and tells us right from wrong."

b) *Agreement*, which focuses on survey questions like "When disagreements occur, we work hard to achieve 'win-win' solutions" and "It is easy to reach consensus, even on difficult issues."

c) *Coordination and integration*, which focuses on survey questions like "People from different parts of the organization share a common perspective" and "There is good alignment of goals across all levels of the organization."

We wanted to dive deeper into the coordination and integration parts of the assessment, given that the company was trying to merge two cultures. So I came up with several open-ended questions that spoke to what mattered most to people from both organizations. We had to identify what values and beliefs they did not want to lose and how could we overlap these areas to come up with a strong unified culture.

The involvement dimension includes the following:

a) *Empowerment*, which focuses on survey questions like "Everyone believes that he or she can have a positive impact" and "Decisions are usually made at the level where the best information is available."

b) *Team orientation*, which focuses on survey questions like "People work like they are part of a team" and "Teamwork is used to get work done, rather than hierarchy."

c) *Capability development*, which focuses on survey questions like "The bench strength is constantly improving" and "There is continuous investment in the skills of all employees."

This was another area where my firm needed to take a deep dive into the details. How did each company view teamwork? What was their orientation toward developing talent? Did employees feel empowered? There were stark differences between the organizations in two areas: (a) one company had a firm belief that people were the organizations greatest asset while the other did not have a strong focus on talent development and (b) one company valued hierarchy and positional power while the other was more diplomatic and had a decentralized structure. This posed a challenge for us. How were we to help them merge the two cultures? We had to convince the CEO what would be the best course moving forward given their strategic priorities around growth and innovation.

The final dimension of the Denison Culture Survey focuses on adaptability. It includes the following:

a) *Creating change*, which focuses on survey questions like "New and improved ways to do work are continually adopted" and "Different parts of the organization often cooperate to create change."

b) *Customer focus*, which focuses on survey questions like "Customer comments and recommendations often leads to changes" and "Customer input directly influences our decisions."

c) *Organizational learning*, which focuses on survey questions like "We view failure as an opportunity for learning and improvement" and "Innovation and risk-taking are encouraged and rewarded."

The adaptability dimension was the most critical area for my firm to focus on. We had to determine if there were major differences with the two cultures around change, customer focus, and organizational learning. The results of the survey were compelling. There were three lessons that we learned. First, both cultures valued the importance of change. People across both companies consistently looked for new ways to drive performance. Employees also valued creativity and leveraging intellectual curiosity to make improvements. Second, both cultures had strong mission-driven values. Employees from both companies wanted to disrupt the industry and accelerate the use of technology for their customers. Lastly, both cultures understood the importance of organizational learning. People strived for continuous growth and development. This would bode well for establishing a culture of innovation. The major differences revolved around how each company viewed talent development and decision-making authority.

When I shared the results with the CEO, he was pleasantly surprised that both companies valued innovation so much. This would make it easy for him to rally people around a unified vision and purpose. He struggled with the hierarchy issue. His company was the one that valued tradition and a top-down approach to management. I had to convince him that moving to a nonhierarchical structure would foster greater teamwork and collaboration. His people had to make the other company's employees feel valued and appreciated.

After some reflection, he brought the leadership teams together from both organizations to outline their path forward. I was impressed with how he laid out his vision for their future. He incorporated key cultural attributes from both companies and worked with his team to develop a collective cultural framework. It took some time for employees to acclimate to the changes, but after six months, we started to see positive improvements. The company had its purpose laid out. People believed in what they were trying to accomplish. Their CEO had fostered an environment of innovation and creativity, and it permeated through all levels of the organization.

Innovative leaders know how to build cultures that bring about change. Their curious and open-minded beliefs resonate with employees at all levels of their organizations. This encourages people to generate new ideas, take risks, and learn from the experiences. They get people to think more broadly, anticipate the future, and take action that drive results. Their flexibility and adaptability inspire people to take chances. Culture building takes times. It's the innovative leaders who invest the time and resources needed to bring about change. When they do this, people start to think differently. They look for opportunities to come up with new ideas. They look for ways to innovate. They take chances because their leaders create the environments for them to do so.

Championing Diversity of Thought

Innovative leaders champion diversity of thought from their people. They look for ways to promote the ideas of others. They are humble and are willing to admit what they don't know. This encourages employees to share their thoughts and perspectives. People have to feel that their insights are valued. When leaders establish an environment where ideas can be cultivated, people take chances. They go out on a limb to think differently. They leverage each other to brainstorm and come up with new ideas.

Rachel, a senior executive in the media and entertainment industry, understood how to unleash the collective ideas of her team. I began coaching her after she was promoted into a new role. Her team was tasked with developing new content for one of their entertainment platforms. The task at hand was large. Her team needed to develop three to four new show concepts for the next year. Given that she was new to her role, she had to take time to understand her people before she could tap into their creative sides. Our coaching development plan focused on three areas. First, she had to learn about the backgrounds and experiences of each of her direct reports. This allowed her to get a thorough understanding on the types of shows and programming each of them had worked on. Second, she needed to bring the team together to outline her vision around innovation.

Third, and this was the most important, she had to create a team culture that promoted collaboration and creativity.

Rachel quickly took action on her first development objective. She started a cadence of having regular one-on-ones with each of her direct reports. She had seven team members, and they all had diverse backgrounds and experiences. Some had worked on reality TV projects. Others had focused on drama. Some had focused on sports and entertainment. Each leader had a unique perspective they brought to the table from these experiences. This was only a start though. She went a step further to more deeply understand how each of her people viewed the industry. She asked questions like "How do we see our viewers evolving in the near future?" "What needs can we anticipate about our customers?" "How can we create new content that could shift the way people view our network?" Her direct reports had many ideas. She took note of all of them and made sure her people felt comfortable brainstorming across any subject matter. This showed them that she was committed to the best ideas, even if they did not come directly from her ways of thinking.

Next, Rachel brought the team together for a group brainstorming session. I had the pleasure of sitting in on this meeting to observe how she was interacting with her team. She started the session with a simple mandate: "Let's create great new content this upcoming year. All ideas are important, and we want to leverage the best insights and experiences of this team." Beginning the discussion in this way opened the door for her people to begin brainstorming. They had white boards all around the room, and each of her people was asked to outline their own ideas. She gave each of them an hour to brainstorm together and then share the ideas with the larger team. I watched people put ideas that were all over the place up on the white boards. Ideas for action and drama shows. Ideas for reality TV shows. Ideas for comedy. Ideas for learning and education. Ideas for sports. Ideas for horror. There was nothing they held back. After an hour, there were close to thirty new ideas that the team had come up with.

Rachel didn't stop there. She had each of her team members report out to the group about what they came up with. Some ideas were out there. The ideas were very different from the types of content the network produced. Rachel never criticized or put down a single idea they shared. She looked for ways to combine ideas and come up with better options. She encouraged the team to challenge each other to flesh out the ideas and get to a better outcome. She applauded their efforts and encouraged them to express each of their viewpoints. By the end of the meeting, the team had narrowed thirty ideas down to eight new show concepts that people could get behind. Rachel let them do the work. She offered her perspective during all the brainstorming but let her people lead the discussion. When we had our next coaching session, I took time to discuss why Rachel let the meeting unfold the way it did. She was quick to point out that throughout her career her managers and mentors encouraged her to be thoughtful and creative. They told her to hold nothing back and think outside the box. She saw how this unleashed her creative capabilities. She wanted to establish this norm with her team. She knew this would have ripple effects down through her people's teams. Championing diversity of thought takes time. People have to feel that they work in a safe environment to tap into their creativity.

Action Steps for Leading with Innovation

Strive for continuous improvements

If you want to be innovative, you have to have a mind-set for continuous improvement. You have to be willing to revisit and refine goals and objectives along the way. Stagnation breeds complacency. Creativity comes from tapping into what's possible. When you're consistently striving for improvements, you're able to prioritize issues and focus the organizational on the most critical levers to drive success. You can strategize about the future and anticipate long-term risks. You have to be willing to be vulnerable and think about things differently. This can be challenging for some leaders. They like to stick to what's tried and tested, missing out on opportunities for accelerating growth of the business. They also are not willing to take calculated, well-thought-out risks. This hinders their teams from driving change.

As a leader, you have to be willing to look at problems from multiple angles and effectively evaluate all viable options. You also have to think outside of your organization. You have to be attuned to the competition. You have to identify potential external threats early on and propose offensive and defensive strategies to meet the needs of the moment. This is the only way for continuous progress and growth. You have to be able to consider the impact of your decisions. What you do today will have an impact on tomorrow.

When I work with clients around innovation, I ask several important questions to focus their efforts on change. First, what is the current state of affairs? Where are you today? What are the needs and concerns of the business? Next, it is all about tomorrow. Where do you want to get to? What's your plan for doing so? How can you leverage others to get there? Lastly, how can you make it happen? What ideas and innovations can you and your team come up with to close the gap? You have to follow these steps in the order they have been laid out to get to the best possible outcomes. If you don't take stock of where you are today, you will not be able to come up with the right improvements to get you where you want to be in the future.

Driving continuous change and improvements takes courage. You have to be a risk-taker. Not a reckless one, though. You need to take calculated risks. How do you do that? You have to spot patterns and trends on a macrolevel. You have to be agile and nimble in anticipating and responding to changes in the operating landscape. You also have to surround yourself around risk-takers. The team that focuses on the right objectives, but has the flexibility to innovate can come up with the right solutions to problems. The team that doesn't have an awareness of what they need to focus on will lose their way. It's that simple. Chart the course and constantly encourage people to do things in new and different ways.

Those who strive for continuous improvement know how to use data and analytics to track progress against objectives. They do not overly rely on their personal experiences. They drive organizational improvements through decisive assessment of issues and then apply deliberate, focused attention to solve problems. Make sure you're doing this in your work. An efficient thinker is quick to focus their team on the most important priorities. You can be structured and organized in your thinking, but encourage people to look for creative solutions rather than accepting the status quo. With innovation and creative thinking, you can't get bogged down in the details. You can't lose sight of the big picture. They say the devil is in the details. Well, with driving change and striving for improvements, sticking to the details slows things down. It prevents progress. You have to create an environment where people can expand upon novel ideas. You can't get in their way or focus on specifics too early.

When you're striving for continuous improvement, take charge in seeking and leveraging new opportunities. Develop a passion and love for the stimulation that comes from intellectual challenges. Learn new subject matter to improve performance. Try to develop new ideas to solve traditional problems. Make decisions based on the best information available, but don't dwell on things too long. Strive to learn new techniques and procedures that will enhance productivity. Don't become wedded to a particular perspective. It will prevent you from considering alternative ideas. Be curious and open-minded. Encourage your people to do the same. This will help your team generate new ideas. It will also create a culture where people are constantly looking for new and better ways to do their work.

Know your audience

Coming up with new and creative ideas is one-half of the equation in driving innovation. The other half is about selling your ideas to others. To do this, you have to know your audience. You have to be able to gauge where people's heads are at and if they are ready to hear what you have to say. If you move too quickly, you will lose your audience and miss out on getting the right buy-in and support from others. I saw this early on in my own career. As a young psychologist and management consultant, I was eager to learn and be successful. One of my first client engagements involved coaching a number of general managers for a retail client. It was my first exposure to executive coaching. I didn't know what I was doing. Earlier that year, I had the opportunity to observe some of the senior partners in our firm coach executives. I picked up what I could but still had so much to learn. With little coaching experience, I was thrown into the deep end and asked to work with close to thirty different general managers over a three-month period.

These coaching engagements were set up a bit differently than most traditional coaching programs. A typical coaching engagement lasts for six months. There are times when it can be nine months or a year, but six months is usually a good starting point. The program I was working on had a slightly different structure. There were to be four coaching sessions per leader over a three-month time frame. This coaching process was part of a larger talent development initiative that the client was delivering. The structure of the sessions was clearly laid out. Certain topics needed to be covered in each session. As I started meeting with the general managers, I quickly realized that a one-size-fit-all approach would not work. Some general managers were new to their roles. Others were seasoned veterans. Some had been promoted up through the ranks. Others had been brought in from other companies. Some had recently assembled new leadership teams. Others had been working with their teams for many years.

As I began to think through ways that I could have a positive impact with each of the leaders, I started to brainstorm ideas. Was there an approach I should take with the new general managers? How should I help the seasoned veterans? What ways could I help leaders who were new to the company? I came up with different coaching processes for each type of leader. After a month, I had several "playbooks" for the different leaders I was working with. I shared the ideas with some of my colleagues but didn't get buy-in and alignment with the account managers who were leading the project. The program was running well on my end until we had to do an internal status meeting with the account managers. I was asked to talk through the protocol that was established for the program. I didn't have the answers they wanted because I had adapted and adjusted my approach without discussing the plan with others.

We had to do some damage control at the corporate level, given that I had strayed from the program. I had missed the opportunity to engage our account managers early on in the process to communicate what I was doing. It was a mistake on my part but taught me a valuable lesson. You need to understand your audience and share your ideas and innovations before taking action. If I had known what the account managers were trying to do at the corporate level, it would have given me the opportunity to share my ideas and perspectives and get their support. Learning this lesson early on in my career has helped me to influence the activities of my clients today. Whenever I am working with leaders on innovation, I make sure that they remember to sell their ideas with others. You can have the best idea possible, but if you don't sell it in the right way at the right time, there could be negative consequences.

Make sure you understand the bigger picture when you're looking to drive innovation. Develop a thorough understanding of your different stakeholders, and keep them apprised of what you are doing. Seek their input on ideas that you come up with. Make sure they feel that their perspectives matter. Incorporate their input into your final plans and actions. Innovation at the organizational level has to have support from many different stakeholders. The leaders who take the time to include others in their thinking tend to be successful at implementing change.

Promote the creativity of others

If you want to build a culture of innovation, you need to unleash the creativity of others. Leaders who give their people the autonomy to think differently get the best ideas from their teams. You have to do this in a smart and calculated way, though. You cannot give people too much freedom. You have to set up guardrails and parameters that people can operate within. I've worked with too many clients who miss this important step, and their teams never get things accomplished. You want people who are inquisitive. You want them to be curious and imaginative. At the same time, you need them to be practical and pragmatic.

Some of the best innovators surround themselves with two types of people. On the one hand, they have people who are visionaries. Those who are quick on their feet and can think big picture. These employees tend to generate lots of ideas. On the other hand, they have people who are realists. They help the team move forward. They can translate ideas into actions. If you have too many of the former, you'll have a team that will not make sensible decisions. They will generate many innovative ideas but won't be able to put them into actions. If you have too many of the latter, you'll have a team that sticks to what's worked in the past. They will execute on the plan but not look for ways to drive continuous improvements.

Take stock of your team. Do you have inquisitive team members? Do you have pragmatic ones? Do you have the idea generators? Do you have the ones who can put thoughts into action? Make sure you have both. Encourage all your people to partner together as ideas are developed and implemented. If you do this, you will be able to rollout successful action plans and then make the necessary adjustments and changes that you need to along the way. That's the beauty of innovation. You don't need to do it all by yourself. You don't even need to be a good innovator. If you get the right people around you, innovation will start to take place on its own. Your job as the leader of the team is to manage the complexity. Make sound resource allocations and prioritize people's work efforts. Reward and celebrate innovation, appropriate risk taking, and driving continuous improvement. When new ideas are brought to the team, probe around to get at the root causes of issues. This will help you create plans for change.

Several years ago, I started working with Roger, a senior executive in the technology industry. He understood how important innovation is for technology. The tech companies that anticipate the future and develop new products and services for their customers are the organizations that thrive. Roger was an innovator, but he was also a great manager of talent. He knew how to bring people onto his team that had different strengths and capabilities. He didn't have to be the one to generate all the new and creative ideas. He wanted people on his team that could take on that responsibility. Our firm helped him identify, select, and onboard several leaders who complemented his skill sets.

Once he had his team in place, he outlined his vision for innovation. He put several cultural pillars in place that would foster an environment that promoted continuous learning and growth. I was impressed with how quickly he was able to get alignment with his team. Part of this was the people he selected. They were all curious and open-minded. The other part was the way he encouraged creativity and diversity of thought from his people. Over the next twelve months, his team developed several new products that would change the landscape for the industry. It was his leadership that helped the team accomplish these goals. He always supported new ideas. He always encouraged the team to debate and discuss ideas. He made sure that once an idea had been fleshed out, they put a plan in place to bring it to life.

Innovative leaders champion the creativity of others. They are not afraid to try new things, make mistakes, and learn from them. They instill this belief in their teams. If you want to unlock the creative potential of your people, make sure you promote their ideas. Make sure you acknowledge both good and bad ideas. Sometimes, the bad ideas are the breeding ground for even better innovations. The thing that matters most is that you create an environment where idea creation is valued and appreciated. Innovation and creativity come when you take action, not just when you have people thinking. Once you start to discuss and talk through ideas, more of them will come. Innovation happens when your team takes actions and works on ideas together.

Evolve or get left behind

We are living in an ever-changing world. Technology keeps advancing regardless of your industry. You have to evolve, or you will get left behind. If you want to be considered an innovative leader, you have to focus your team on the future. You have to be able to prioritize the right things and keep people focused on the bigger picture. Leaders who get stuck in tradition or think what worked yesterday will work today fail. I've seen this happen with some of my clients. They get fixated on what has brought success in the past. This causes them to lose sight of what's possible and miss out on opportunities to learn and grow.

162

Early in my career, I worked with a medical devices company that had a rich heritage and history with their customers. The executive leadership team had been successful for many years sticking to the basics and doing what they knew best. This worked for a long period of time. The culture they created did not value change. They believed that what they did yesterday would continue to work for their customers in the present and in the future. I was brought in to help the organization identify and assess external talent. Given that I had done a lot of work in the medical devices sector, I explained how their competitors were assessing and onboarding new leaders. We talked through the state of the industry, where talent was being sourced from, and the types of leaders they needed to grow the business. At a surface level, they understood that they needed to adapt and grow. However, as I continued to work with their CHRO, it quickly became apparent that the CEO did not want the company to evolve and change.

Before we even started assessing candidates, I knew the company needed to change their leadership competency framework. The skills and behaviors that made them successful in the past were not going to work in the future. Although I advocated strongly for changing their competency model, the CEO wouldn't budge. He felt he knew best about the types of leaders who would thrive in their culture. This may have been true in the past, but they needed to think differently about the types of people who would challenge the organization to grow. Over a two-year period, I assessed close to twenty senior executives for different roles across the enterprise. Many of these candidates had the talents and capabilities that would take the company to the next level. Going against our recommendations, they hired very few of these candidates. Instead, the company hired people who fit the bill. They onboarded leaders who wouldn't challenge the system and get people to think differently.

As you can imagine, this started to have a negative effect on their ability to drive sales growth. Their competitors were developing new products and services that were meeting the ever-changing needs of their customers. They were sticking to what worked well in the past. They didn't do what was necessary to evolve the business.

The company continued to struggle more and more. In the end, they were acquired by a larger organization, and the entire leadership team was removed. They missed the mark on when and where they needed to change. I learned a valuable lesson from this experience that I take into all of my client work today. You have to be flexible and adaptable. You have to be willing to have an unflinching confrontation of the external changes that require internal translation and course correction. You have to identify potential threats to the business early on and propose strategies to stay relevant and compete in the market. You have to consider the impact of market trends on the organization and be willing to drive change. You have to do what is necessary to evolve.

Make sure you're always attuned to what's going on around you. Be willing to make tough strategic decisions based on objective analysis of facts, data, and lessons learned. See through complexity and consider alternatives to finding the best possible path forward. You have to be willing to take action and make the necessary changes to improve processes and procedures. If you do this, you will keep your company on the cutting edge. You'll create a culture of growth where people are consistently looking to innovate and try new things.

WISDOM

Blessed is the man who finds wisdom, the
man who gains understanding.
—Proverbs 3:13

It was the second semester of my first year in college. The previous semester I had taken the standard introduction to psychology course that most undergraduates take as an elective. I knew I wanted to be a psychology major but didn't know what area I wanted to specialize in. The course covered all the areas of psychology (e.g., clinical, social, school, experimental). Each was interesting to learn about, but I found myself drawn to industrial-organizational (I-O) psychology. As an athlete, I was fascinated by leadership and teamwork. When I learned there was a discipline of psychology that focused solely on these areas, I fell in love. At the time, I had no idea what an I-O psychologist was but was drawn to the study of motivation, goal setting, and performance.

I signed up for an I-O psychology course not knowing what to expect. On the first day of class, I was eager to learn. I knew some of the professors in the psychology department but didn't know who would be teaching this course. In walked a professor, dressed in a three-piece suit. Now most professors don't dress like this. Some of them dress like students. He introduced himself as Dr. Roberts and said that he had just come from a client meeting in New York City. He explained to the class that he was coaching a senior executive who had just been promoted into an important role for an organization. This sparked my interest. What was a coach? I knew about coaches in sports but had no idea that business leaders worked with coaches. He told us a little about what a coach was before he took us through the syllabus for the semester. We were to cover things like job analysis, performance appraisals, selection, leadership, team effectiveness, motivation, and organizational development. All the subjects seemed appealing to me. I was excited about the prospects of learning about each of these subjects.

Over the course of the next three months, my passion for I-O psychology grew. I learned about internal consultants and the work they typically do in HR. I learned about external management consultants and how they work with companies to support the growth and development of employees. What stood out to me most was the variety of jobs and opportunities that existed for I-O psychologists. At the end of the semester, I wrote Dr. Roberts a letter. The premise was simple. I wanted to first thank him for what he taught in the class, but I also wanted to see if there were any opportunities to learn more from him. I remember writing the letter being eager to learn. Little did I know it would set the stage for finding my true calling.

Several weeks after I sent the letter to Dr. Roberts, I received a call from one of his graduate assistants. Dr. Roberts was going to be presenting some of his research at the American Psychological Association's annual conference, and he wanted me to attend. I jumped at the opportunity. The conference was held in New York City that year. Dr. Roberts was presenting in the morning on a topic called EQ. This was right after Daniel Goleman had written his book *Emotional Intelligence*. As I sat in the audience, I was mesmerized by the subject matter. Dr. Roberts discussed the importance of self-awareness and why it was critical to the success of any leader. He discussed how understanding the emotions of others can have a positive impact on how leaders motivate and inspire their employees. He talked about case studies with some of his clients and how managing one's emotions can make or break a leader. After the presentation, I came up to him to ask some follow-up questions, and he invited me out to lunch that afternoon.

Over lunch, we talked about many topics. From emotional intelligence to being an I-O psychologist to working with leaders, he explained the different types of opportunities in the field. As a young college student, I was impressed by his knowledge and wisdom. Dr.

Roberts had over thirty years of consulting experience, and I knew I needed to learn all I could from him. At the end of our lunch, he asked me what I wanted to do with my future. I had made up my mind that I wanted to be an I-O psychologist! He told me about an accelerated bachelor's and master's degree program that was offered at my university and encouraged me to apply for the program. He told me that if I was accepted into the program, he had a spot for me on his team as one of his graduate assistants. I left New York City that day on a mission to get into the program and work directly with him.

The next year, I was accepted into the program and began working with Dr. Roberts. Working as his graduate assistant, I learned many things. I learned a lot about the field of I-O psychology. I learned how to teach a college-level course. I learned how to navigate relationships with different leaders across the university. All these things were important to my development. However, I learned the most through one-on-one conversations we would have at the start of each day. We would get together early in the morning before classes started and just talk about life. Many of the conversations focused on my future. Did I want to start my career after completing my master's degree? What type of work did I want to do after college? Did I want to teach at a university? Did I want to secure an internal role within an organization? Did I want to work as an external management consultant? Did I want to get my doctorate in I-O psychology?

What was most powerful about our discussions was the knowledge and wisdom Dr. Roberts shared about his career. After many conversations, I made the decision to move forward with pursuing my doctorate degree. At that point in time, I knew little about the types of graduate I-O programs across the country. Dr. Roberts worked with me to narrow down the list. He knew so much information about the different schools and made strong recommendations on where I should apply. The application process was intense. I applied to ten different schools. Some were in the top ten of the nation for I-O psychology. Others were at the midtier level. I wasn't sure where I would end up. After several months of hard work (e.g., GRE exams, school visits, submitting applications), I was accepted into one of the premier universities in the country. I was thrilled that

I would be taking the next step in my academic career in pursuit of my doctorate degree.

A month before I received my master's degree, I sat down with Dr. Roberts for one of our regular one-on-one conversations. Little did I know it would be one of the most memorable and impactful conversations of my life. He knew that I was a hard worker and dedicated to my craft. He also knew that I was a perfectionist and that I wanted to do all I could to succeed. He told me four things that helped guide me through the next twenty years of my career. First, he told me to strive for excellence, not perfection. Over his career, he had worked with many leaders who were not able to make this distinction. Those who had to control everything ended up burning out or failing. If I wanted to be a successful management psychologist, I would have to learn to do my best and let the results speak for themselves. At first, this was a hard pill to swallow. At the time, everything I did had to be perfect. It took me many years to understand the wisdom in this lesson. Life experience will do that to you.

Second, we talked about getting my doctorate degree. He told me that it was a great honor to get the degree but that it was simply getting my ticket swiped. He advised me to finish the degree in the most efficient time frame possible. I remember him saying, "Don't dwell too much on having to get everything right. Do what you need to do to get the degree and start your career. Make sure you learn life lessons in graduate school. It's not just about getting the degree." I took this to heart, and it helped shape my outlook on how I approached the process of completing my PhD.

Third, he taught me that "you never get a second chance to make a first impression." If I wanted to have a lasting impact on people, the *how* was just as important as the *what*. He was a firm believer in dressing to impress. He also taught me that relationships matter more than knowledge or expertise. He told me, "The world is filled with smart people. Those who can build relationships and effectively influence people have the greatest success." That has stuck with me throughout my career. It helped me secure my first consulting role after I completed my doctorate degree. The firm I ended up starting my career with typically hired seasoned consultants, not young professionals right out of graduate school. It was the way I carried myself and how I built relationships with the firm's leaders during the selection process that helped secure me a role with the firm.

Lastly, he told me to become a lifelong learner. Just because I was getting my doctorate didn't mean I would know everything. There would be opportunities to learn things from people in all walks of life. He advised me that once I started consulting to find good mentors. Identifying people who were successful would be critical to my growth and development as a professional. I've applied this lesson to all the work that I do. From the CEO down to the executive assistant, there are life lessons that we can learn from different types of people. He taught me to be mindful of this and to engage people with a curious and inquisitive mindset.

I learned many things from Dr. Roberts. The knowledge and wisdom that he had acquired over a long consulting career has helped shape the organizational psychologist I am today. It wasn't just about his intellect and intelligence. He understood how today's decisions have an impact on tomorrow. He set a tone for learning from both successes and failures. He had a broad and deep understanding of different industries, sectors, and business environments. He had exceptional business acumen and knew how to apply it to different situations and circumstances. He was a quick learner who understood critical success drivers of business, people, and culture. He could draw parallels and linkages from past experiences and use them in the work that he did. It was an honor and privilege to work as his protégé. It has made me a better consultant and trusted advisor to all the clients I work with today.

Why IQ Is Not Enough

In the field of I-O psychology, the concept of IQ, which is supposed to be a rough measure of general intelligence (mostly hereditary), has a robust history of research behind it. In fact, it's one of the most concretely tested measures in the field. The correlations it shows are comparatively sturdy across a number of different variables. However, having a high IQ does not equate to having wisdom. Intelligence refers to one's potential to acquire and apply knowledge. Knowledge is the theoretical or practical understanding of a particular subject. Fundamentally, it is an abstract concept because the definition of *intelligence* is determined by social circumstances and the availability of scientific information. It is important to acknowledge that intelligence is linked to one's capabilities, more so than what they already know.

In terms of functioning in organizational settings, intelligent people are able to effortlessly pick up new skills, effectively solve problems, and comprehend complex ideas. Intelligent leaders can spot patterns and trends with customers and competitors. They are strategic and nimble in anticipating and responding to changes in the market. They also tend to possess strong analytical capabilities. Leaders with high IQ can evaluate arguments based on the relevance and strength of the evidence supporting them. They can define the basic elements of most problems and situations clearly and objectively. They build arguments that integrate several pieces of relevant information from diverse perspectives. They can draw accurate conclusions from information in most situations.

Wisdom is considerably more difficult to conceptualize than intelligence. There are a variety of unpredictable factors that contribute to a leader being considered wise. You cannot test for wisdom by administering an IQ test. Wisdom encompasses obtaining knowledge through direct experience and critical judgment. Inevitably, the experiences of leaders are objectively and subjectively different. Characteristically, wisdom is the ability to determine the truth and validity of accumulated knowledge. It is usually developed by undergoing negative and positive experiences that develop one's values and moral compass. Wisdom is the pairing of a leader's accumulated knowledge over time and their ability to synthesize this knowledge using their understanding of the world around them.

Both intelligence and wisdom are centered on the idea of accumulating and utilizing knowledge. In most situations, it's usually impossible to be exclusively intelligent or exclusively wise. Most leaders exhibit characteristics of both within their areas of expertise. Intelligence and wisdom are linked to the operation of the mind. The mind is a powerful and complex system—one that holds the potential to shift and change depending on social and environmental factors. Although intelligence and wisdom are two distinct characteristics of the mind, IQ in and of itself is not enough for a leader to be truly successful. Because wisdom is an undeniably subjective character trait, it has to take shape over time. Wise leaders learn from their experiences—both positive and negative—and can adjust their behaviors based on these factors.

A leader who is intelligent is capable of easily obtaining and using knowledge. A wise leader knows how to acquire and use knowledge based on the accumulation of their experiences over time. They learn from their mistakes and make adjustments as time progresses. Leaders with high IQ understand how to solve problems from an analytical perspective. They can interpret evidence objectively. Leaders with a lot of wisdom can read between the lines and understand how to obtain a deep, multifaceted understanding of their environment. They are skilled at defining and redefining issues based on what they know from the past and the possibilities of the future. Intelligent leaders understand knowledge and how it contributes to their work. Wise leaders know how to apply knowledge to real-life situations where factors like people and relationships come into play.

Intelligence and wisdom are abstract concepts that are difficult to grasp without understanding their manifestation in the real world. It's easier to conceptualize the difference between IQ and wisdom when the concepts are applied to practical examples. People will often attribute characteristics of intelligence to successful figures like Elon Musk, the cofounder of Tesla. His understanding of his environment and the evolution of automobiles inspired him and his colleagues to build electric vehicles and create a clean energy company. His high IQ was a catalyst for his success.

On the other hand, wisdom is often displayed by progressive, successful leaders like former President Barack Obama. Obama is the type of leader who related to the world by understanding the variation of possibilities and opportunities that contribute to obtaining knowledge. He possessed high self-awareness and was a firm believer in striving for what is right. Wise leaders have a holistic understanding of their environment and often use their knowledge to enact long-lasting, meaningful change. To be a successful leader, you have to be more than just intelligent. You have to know how to use your intelligence and your life experiences to have a positive impact on your people and your organization. Intelligence may be obtained through hereditary, but it is wisdom that plays a greater role in the success of any leader.

The Value of Information Sharing

Wise leaders understand the importance of sharing information. They can translate an understanding of industry, customers, and competitors to broad strategic choices and then operationalize this information into compelling initiatives and priorities for others. They don't hold on to information that can help advance the agenda of the organization. They think about the business from a holistic, systemic lens rather than through a narrow perspective. They elicit the guidance and input from others. They work with others to anticipate the downstream impact of decisions on customers, employees, and financials. By sharing information with key stakeholders, they can sift through competing data points and prioritize the right set of action items.

Wise leaders invest time in learning new information. They aspire to develop a deep understanding of their business. This involves teamwork. You cannot learn and grow without sharing information. There are different types of information sharing. Some types focus on the financials and key business outcomes. When leaders are well-informed on the metrics that are driving performance and productivity, they can make accurate decisions to grow the business. Other types focus on people and talent. When leaders understand their talent, they can make important strategic decisions about people. This enables them to effectively plan for succession and tailor the right development opportunities for employees.

As a senior executive, you have to lead with a global mindset. You have to think outside of your cultural perspective. This takes time. That is why it is critical for leaders to stay well-informed and up to date on changing external factors impacting their business. When leaders share information with one another, they are more open to taking calculated risks. They can evaluate outcomes and make adjustments based on all the relevant data available. Information sharing also opens up opportunities for new ideas to be developed. It helps leaders identify ways of challenging existing processes and procedures. It helps leaders discern ideas from an array of possibilities. They can challenge established ways of thinking in a constructive manner. It helps them stay on the cutting edge of customer needs and market trends.

When working with my clients, I am always looking for the leaders who are willing to share information openly. It creates a positive, more impactful dynamic for any of our individual, team, or organizational programs. When leaders share information, it helps to inform how we can best meet their needs. One of my current clients is exceptional at providing the context and background for the work of her team. When I started working with her, she painted a broad picture of the key strategic objectives for her organization. She talked about the history and legacy of their work. She outlined how her team's goals and initiatives fit into the larger landscape for the company. I thought this was just to provide context for me as her coach. This was not the case. She did this with all of her colleagues. She never asked people to take action without communicating how their work tied into the bigger picture. By sharing information with others, she garnered greater support and commitment from her people. It also created a culture and environment where her people did the same thing with one another. When employees are well-informed about how their work ties into the bigger picture, they are able to get to desired outcomes quicker. That is why information sharing is so important. It takes trust and commitment for leaders to share information openly.

There are times when leaders need to hold on to information. Certain initiatives or special projects can be communicated on a needs-to-know basis. This often takes place when there are major organizational changes or restructuring. However, I have found that when leaders can share information, it is usually good to be open and transparent. Employees are more productive when their work has meaning. Meaning comes from understanding the broader landscape. Information sharing also fosters an environment that promotes continuous learning. It enables people to develop and grow. It is linked to innovation as well. When cross-functional teams are working on new initiatives and readily share information, new ideas are developed. Wise leaders understand the power in sharing information. It connects the dots for their teams. It helps employees take a hands-on approach to their work. It helps people develop new skills quickly when confronted with challenges or difficult circumstances.

Leveraging the Experiences of Others

Wise leaders go out of their way to leverage the experiences of others. They know that they don't have to have all the answers. They understand how to solicit input and insights from people. It takes humility to go to others for counsel, guidance, and support. Because wisdom is developed over time, the wise leaders are always looking for ways to learn. Leveraging the experiences of others can take place in many different ways. There is learning by observation. Most leadership advisory firms use this model to train new consultants. The new hire will shadow or partner with a seasoned veteran to learn the craft. This also helps give new consultants a chance to learn and acclimate to the firm's culture. Early in my career, I was paired with several mentors that helped shape the way that I do my consulting work. There were things I picked up from each of them. I learned how to interact with clients at the start of an engagement. I learned how to follow up on leads and sell new work. I learned how to assess senior executives—for both selection and development. I learned how to be an executive coach. As I continued to learn from each of my mentors, I began to understand how to be an effective management psychologist. It took years to develop the right skills, but the insights I learned from others helped me to establish a strong foundation.

There is also learning by doing. One of the best ways to learn new information is to work side-by-side with someone who is exceptionally skilled at their craft. You get a front-row seat to the action. I see this a lot in the retail sector. When new sales or marketing leaders are brought on to a team, they get a chance to partner with colleagues within their area of responsibility. They also get to work cross-functionally with others. The wise leader will jump at these opportunities. It helps them accelerate their knowledge and growth. They also get a chance to get their hands dirty. When they are working with others, there are more opportunities to learn from mistakes. They get to operate in a safe environment where others can help pick up the slack if they miss something.

We touched on mentoring earlier, but it is important to reiterate its importance here. Wise leaders learn the most when they are paired with strong mentors. Sometimes, this happens by decisions the organization makes, and other times it happens more naturally. I believe the natural partnerships that take place over time have the greatest impact. When the relationship between mentor and mentee forms organically, there is a deeper sense of trust that takes place. In these situations, the mentee is more likely to lean on their mentor for support. However, for the mentee to get the most out of the relationship, they have to be proactive and hungry to learn. They also have to take the initiative to get the most out of the relationship.

When I work with companies to help develop mentoring programs, there are several factors that the mentors and mentees need to put in place. First, the mentors have to set clear time-management expectations at the beginning of the relationship. The mentees need to realize that their mentor's time is valuable. Putting in place a consistent rhythm helps to structure the time spent together. Second, the mentor and mentee need to be clear about what they want to get out of the relationship. Does the mentee want to increase their knowledge in a particular area? Do they want to learn how to better navigate the culture of the company? Do they want to sharpen their skills in a specific discipline? The mentee needs to know what they want to do before they go out and seek a mentor. For the mentor, they need to manage expectations by being clear about what they can offer. When a mentee is vague about their goals, a good mentor will challenge them to be specific about their desired outcomes.

Third, mentorship should be energizing for both parties. The mentor should get excited by sharing what they know, and the mentee should be committed to learning and growth. This is where the chemistry between the two comes into play. Do they have similar personality styles? How do they relate to one another? What do they share in common? If there are some similarities between the two, the mentee is more likely to tap into what the mentor knows. Lastly, the two have to acknowledge the work that goes into the partnership. For the mentees, this means having a curious and inquisitive mind-set. They have to ask questions and thank the mentor for their guidance and stewardship. For the mentors, it's about going the extra mile to help bring out the best in their mentee.

Wise leaders don't need to possess superior intellectual and analytical powers. Don't get me wrong. These are helpful, but it is the leaders who have an appetite for learning who grow the most. When they go out of their way to learn from others, they sharpen their skill sets. The eager learners who are willing to immerse themselves in acquiring knowledge have the greatest success in the long run. By listening to the experiences of others, they can draw appropriate parallels and linkages from the past. This helps inform their decision-making. It creates sustainability in the work of their teams.

Feedback also plays a critical role in the process. Wise leaders solicit feedback from others. They want to get better at what they do, and they're not afraid of constructive criticism. Some of the most successful leaders whom I have worked with are constantly looking for input and advice from others. They are open to new ideas. They take the feedback with an open mind and make changes when and where it is necessary. This takes courage and a willingness to admit what one does not know. This is where wise leaders differentiate themselves from others. They are resourceful and have the ability to put into practice what they have learned. By demonstrating the willingness to learn and the flexibility to adapt their approach, they give themselves the best opportunity to maximize their talent.

Failure:
Life's Greatest Teacher

Wise leaders learn from setbacks and failures. They are persistent in pursuing their dreams despite obstacles and challenges. Throughout history, there have been many leaders who have failed before they ever succeeded. Failure can have one of two effects on a leader. It can paralyze some from trying new things and taking chances. It can inspire others to continue to strive toward their goals and objectives. When leaders fail, it makes them question everything, right down to the very heart of who they are and what they believe they're called to do. Failure, as much as it hurts, is a necessary part of life. The wise leaders understand this. It's the pathway to people's dreams and desires.

Many of the most successful and famous people in the world have endured some of the biggest failures in life. They have failed repeatedly, but it does not deter their efforts. They have learned how to get back up and try again. They didn't throw in the towel and quit. They got up and kept going. That's what it takes to succeed. Failure makes wise leaders better. It allows leaders to reach new understandings and epiphanies on life, business, and the people all around them. It's one thing to talk about failure at a theoretical level. It's far more beneficial to look at some of the most successful people who've failed. It is far easier to rely on their experiences and learn what they have had to endure to achieve their dreams.

Perhaps one of the most famous examples of succeeding through failure is Thomas Edison, the American inventor and entrepreneur. Edison went through thousands of iterations to make his dream of inventing a commercially viable incandescent lightbulb. At one point, he was asked by a reporter whether he felt like a failure after so many failed attempts. He responded by saying, "I have not failed ten thousand times. I have not failed once. I have succeeded in proving that those ten thousand ways would not work. When I have eliminated the ways that will not work, I will find the way that will work." This faith and desire to succeed is what motivated Edison. It took great wisdom to understand that his failed attempts weren't true failure. It was just a setback to set him up for the real success.

Michael Jordan, who many believe is the greatest basketball player of all time, is credited with once saying, "I've missed more than nine thousand shots in my career. I've lost almost three hundred games. Twenty-six times, I've been trusted to make the game-winning shot and missed. I've failed over and over and over again in my life. And that is why I succeed." It takes wisdom to believe that. Where other basketball players may look at this as failure, it motivated him. Michael experienced failure early on in life, and it taught him a valuable lesson about being successful. As a high school basketball player, he was cut from the varsity basketball team. At the time, it was a devastating setback. He cried after he saw that his name was not on the roster. This could have prevented him from striving for excellence. Instead of giving up, it motivated him to work harder. Every time he thought about stopping, he would picture that list without his name on it.

In the media and entertainment industry, Oprah Winfrey is considered a great success story. She has built an empire over her career. However, things did not start off that way. After college, she moved to Baltimore, Maryland, to coanchor the news but was later removed by the producers because they felt she was "unfit" for television. This didn't stop Oprah. The failure didn't prevent her from getting back up and trying again. In 1983, she took over a fledging show called *AM Chicago*, which would later become the *Oprah Winfrey* show. She became the highest-ranked talk show in Chicago. Today, she is a multibillionaire and has had a major impact on a large part of the world.

In the technology industry, few can argue the brilliance and talent of Steve Jobs. Jobs was responsible for creating one of the most renowned and successful companies in the world. Yet Jobs's life was filled with failures. Before fame ever graced him and his name became synonymous with success, he suffered through an enormous number of setbacks. In 1976, Jobs cofounded Apple Computers with his friend Steven Wozniak. The company was highly successful early on. However, in 1983, Jobs hired John Scully from Pepsi as CEO to help the company. It ended up being one of the worst decisions he had ever made. After a disagreement with Scully and a foiled plan by Jobs to oust the new CEO, Jobs was removed from the company by the board. He took five employees and started a new business venture, NeXT. At the time, Jobs felt like a failure. The company he started had been taken away from him. That disheartening period helped embolden Jobs. While Apple was fledging and would eventually be on the verge of bankruptcy, NeXT thrived. Ultimately, NeXT was acquired by Apple in 1997, bringing Jobs back into the fold.

Soon thereafter, he developed some of the greatest technologies of the twenty-first century—the main one being the iPhone.

In the film industry, Walt Disney is regarded as developing one of the most famous companies in the world throughout history. However, Disney's road to success wasn't easy; it was paved with a number of setbacks, obstacles, and failures. In 1919, Disney took a job with the *Kansas City Star*, the local newspaper. He was fired by the editor for lacking imagination and having no good ideas. Later, Disney started a company called Laugh-O-Gram, producing cartoon animations. His biggest client at the time was Newman's theaters, one of the largest theater chains. However, his success with Laugh-O-Gram was short-lived. The money earned didn't provide enough income to keep the company afloat, and in 1923, it declared bankruptcy. Disney then relocated to Hollywood where he worked with his brother to form Disney Brothers Studio. The company later became known as the Walt Disney Company but still struggled for close to five years. In 1928, Disney created Mickey Mouse, and things began to take off for the company. Had Disney given up at any point in the journey, the company would not exist today.

In the automotive industry, Henry Ford, who is credited with starting one of the most profitable automotive companies in the world, failed numerous times before reaching success. Early in his career, Ford worked for the Edison Illuminating Company, where in 1893 he was promoted to chief engineer. It was around this time that Ford started experimenting with gasoline engines. It took him over six years to build a self-propelled vehicle. There were many setbacks and failure along the way. In 1899, Ford founded the Detroit Automotive Company. Two years later, the company failed after an inability to pay back a loan to the Dodge brothers. Due to inefficiencies in the design of his vehicle, the company ceased operations dealing a stealthy blow to Ford. However, he did not give up. He learned valuable lessons from his failure and kept on pursuing his dream. It wasn't until 1903, at the age of forty, that Ford gave it one final shot. He founded the Ford Motor Company, which would later become one of the most well-known brands in the automotive industry. Today, the Ford name is synonymous with automobiles. In fact, while the assembly line existed prior to Ford's arrival on the scene, he created a car that was affordable by the everyday family. This helped develop what was to become the largest boom in the automotive industry.

Wise leaders never give up. They take what they can from failures and push forward. I would argue that a leader isn't truly successful until they first have failed. It ignites something inside and brings out the best in great leaders. It inspires them to refocus their efforts and try again. It fuels their passion and desire to win. When wise leaders fail, they learn to take educated risks in trying something new and different. Failure also strengthens one's resilience. You have to have thick skin when it comes to failure. When leaders understand that failure is not the end but is simply a means to get to their desired outcomes, they're able to drive future success. Failure may be painful in the moment, but the truly wise leaders learn from negative experiences and move forward.

Action Steps for Leading with Wisdom

Surround yourself with wise people

If you want to gain wisdom, surround yourself with wise people. Find those who possess knowledge—knowledge of the things you want to learn, knowledge of the things you do not know. You have to use good judgment and discernment when you're identifying whom you want to learn from. I learned this at a young age. There were so many things I had to learn about the field of organizational psychology. Therefore, I was thoughtful in how I put together my list of people whom I wanted to learn from. I selected people who understood the rich history of our field—those who understood leadership, team effectiveness, motivation, and organizational development. I also went outside my area of expertise to find people who were successful in life. I looked for leaders of companies that I admired. I looked for sports figures who could teach me something unique about discipline and perseverance. I read about leaders throughout history—people in politics, the arts, the sciences, and entertainment. When it comes to wisdom, you have to think broadly. You can't be narrow in your thinking. You can't have tunnel vision.

Take time to think about how you want to grow. Every year I set goals for myself, and I look to find people who will help me accomplish my objectives. I've made it a habit of setting goals in a variety of areas. I set goals on a personal level—goals around my health and fitness. Then I go out and find people who are successful in that space. For example, over a decade ago, I became fascinated with long-distance running. I set a goal to run a marathon. I read up on how to train properly for a race. I made sure to study people who had done it successfully and reached out to them for advice and guidance. It takes time and effort to learn from others. You have to have an appetite for growth and a willingness to stretch yourself.

In my professional life, I've made it a habit of studying leaders. Yes, I work with them all the time. I've become a trusted advisor to many of them, but I also learn what I can from each individual. I've learned the most from my CEO clients. CEOs have tough jobs. There are blessings and burdens to being the CEO. Over the last twenty years, I've found that CEOs can affect change more than any other leader in their companies. Although CEOs and presidents of organizations sit in the highest seat of authority, they are called to serve others. They have to set the right example for their people. Their actions speak more than their words. CEOs are blessed with ability to influence. They direct the actions and efforts of others. They can unleash the power and potential of people. At the same time, they deal with the burden of responsibility. They are responsible for the safety and well-being of their employees. One wrong decision by a CEO can have detrimental effects at all levels of an organization.

If you're early in your career, surrounding yourself with the right people is critical to your long-term success. When I work with high potentials, I have them answer five important questions. First, you need to have an idea of where you want to go in your career. Do you aspire to be a leader in your industry? Do you want to bring about change for your organization? Do you have a novel idea or solution that can help others? Getting clear on the path you want to take helps you narrow down the types of people you want to work around. Second, I have them list their strengths and development areas. What do you do really well? What are the best talents and skills that you bring to the table? Where do you struggle? What areas do you want to get better? The mistake people make at this stage is that they only look for people who have strengths in their areas of development. It's a mistake to do this. You want to find role models who share your strengths just as much as you want to find those who excel in your weak areas. Some of my clients have learned the most from working with those who are exceptionally skilled in their strength areas.

Third, I want them to think about people. Leadership is about the impact you have on others. It's about how you help others maximize their potential. So I want them to get a good understanding of how they work with their colleagues. Are you a good team player? Do you take the lead on projects or assignments? Do you take time to mentor and help others grow? The higher a leader moves up in the organization, the less their technical skills matter. It becomes more about how you can get things accomplished through others. That is why it is so important to get an understanding of how to partner with colleagues.

Fourth, I want to find out if they're inquisitive and intellectually curious. Do you have an appetite for learning? Do you take time to listen to the insights and experiences of others? Do you make learning a lifelong pursuit? When high potentials have a desire to learn and grow, they are more likely to seek out experiences that will broaden their horizons. You cannot grow if you're not willing to learn. Lastly, I ask people what they want their legacy to be. What do you want to be known for? What is the mark that you want to leave on others? What is the impact you want to have on the business and the organization? Your legacy matters. The most successful leaders leave a trail behind them. They inspire others to drive change.

Make sure the people you surround yourself with will help you grow. Be humble in the process. It's okay to admit what you do not know. It's okay to reach out to others for help. As I mentioned earlier, wisdom takes place over time. What you're learning today will impact you tomorrow. It will help in your decision-making. It will help you take educated risks. It will open you to new ideas and ways of doing things. Put a great deal of energy behind learning new things. Sometimes, the little things you learn today can have a tremendous impact down the road.

Transfer your knowledge: pay it forward

As you learn and grow, it's important to share your knowledge, expertise, and experiences with others. It's just as important for you to learn as it is for others to do so. Wise leaders understand that when they transfer knowledge to their people, the entire organization gets better. You cannot develop your skills in a vacuum. People learn best when they do it together. You would be surprised how the insights you've accumulated over your career can have such strong impact on others. Take time to share what you know. You can do this strategically by identifying people whom you want to groom. You can also do it in a simple and informal manner. Some of the best conversations where I have shared information with others happened organically. I can be out to lunch with a colleague, and we end up talking about a topic that can help them grow.

You can also transfer knowledge to others by working alongside of them. Having people shadow you or just observe what you do can play an even more important role than what you tell them directly. In our firm's early years, I witnessed this firsthand with several of our new consultants. When we brought each of them into the firm, there was a steep learning curve. They had to learn about each of our service offerings. That was easy the part. They could acquire that knowledge by carefully studying our website and our marketing materials. The challenge was teaching them how to interact with clients. These types of skills are not taught in graduate school. You learn the technical skills there—how to write, how to put your thoughts together in clear and succinct manner, and how to think critically and solve problems. We had to teach them how to deliver and sell work.

The first task was getting them to understand how we do our work. I made sure each of our senior partners took one of the new consultants under their wings. The new team members got to shadow their work for the first six months. During that process, they learned how to coach executives, how to do a selection assessment interview, how do conduct a team effectiveness engagement, and how to conduct a 360-degree assessment. Our model for learning and transfer of knowledge is simple. A new consultant will watch how one of our senior partners does the work. This can take several months depending on the type of work or project. We have regular debriefing sessions after we meet with our clients. We talk them through our approach, answer questions, and discuss the engagement.

Once they've established a foundation of understanding, we have them work side-by-side with our senior partners to deliver new work. They will play an active role in coaching or conducting an assessment. They get to interact and work with our clients while being guided and supervised with a seasoned consultant. This phase of the process can take several months as well. The last phase is letting them take on their own engagements. By this time, they have learned what we do and have worked together with a senior partner to deliver work. They take on assignments that will enable them to stretch and grow. They have their mentors for guidance and support, but they're given the freedom to practice what they've learned.

We follow the same procedure for teaching them how to sell work. They get a front row seat into how we engage and work with prospective clients. They help to put together the proposal decks and marketing materials. In time, they are allowed to play an active role in the sales meetings. We also encourage them to look to expand work in our current clients. This is a safe environment for offering new services to help support the ongoing needs of our clients. Lastly, they are ready to go out and solicit new clients. We trust the work that they have put toward learning these skills and give them the autonomy to perform. By allowing our new team members to work side-by-side with our firm's leaders, they acquire the skills needed to be successful consultants. Wise leaders should do the same with their people.

I've seen wise leaders in action with many of the organizations that I work with. A few years ago, I was asked to coach a high-potential leader for a telecommunications company. Joe was a sharp individual and had an appetite for learning. Prior to our work together, he had spent two years as the chief of staff to a president of one of the company's divisions. In this role, he learned about all different aspects of the business. He was responsible for coordinating projects and working alongside leaders from sales, marketing, operations, HR, finance, and IT. This exposure allowed him to connect with people from all walks of life. What I admired about Joe was that he always asked questions. He was curious and wanted to know how each of the respective leaders did their work. He shared information openly across the division. He leveraged experiences from different leaders, which helped inform his decision-making. That role prepared him for broader leadership responsibilities.

Our coaching engagement began shortly after he was promoted into vice president of retail sales. In this role, he had responsibility for all aspects of the business. He had a team reporting to him that covered sales, operations, HR, and finance. Given his experience as a chief of staff, he had a deep understanding of how all these parts needed to operate. I was asked to work with him to help drive alignment with his new leadership team. What I learned quickly about Joe is that he placed the highest value on relationships and partnering with others. He took time to learn about what his people knew but also shared the things that he had learned earlier in his career. He worked side-by-side with his direct reports. He transferred the knowledge he had learned to help make them a better team. He encouraged his people to do the same with their teams. Within six months, he had a team that had a shared vision of the future. More importantly, they consistently leveraged one another to help support the growth of the business.

When it comes to wisdom, make sure you pay it forward with your people. The valuable lessons you have learned can help others grow and improve. This not only makes your team better, but it creates a culture where people are willing to teach others. Wise leaders understand that working together is what makes organizations successful. They aren't afraid to share what they have learned. Some of the most successful companies thrive because people take time to learn from one another. They understand that the collective knowledge, insights, and wisdom of their people is what drive results and propels their business into the future.

BRINGING IT ALL TOGETHER

Leaders are not born; they are made. And they are made
just like anything else, through hard work. And that's
the price we'll have to pay to achieve that goal.
—Vince Lombardi

Leadership is a journey, not a destination. Although we all are born with talents, skills, and capabilities, leadership development takes time. You have to be willing to put in the hard work and effort if you want to grow as a leader. Some of the best leaders make it a habit to continuously learn. They understand that there are always new things they can add to their leadership toolkit. At the same time, they are curious and look for ways to consistently stay on their game. I look for these traits and personality factors when I work with my clients. The leader who has an appetite to grow is the leader who gets the best out of their personal development.

We live in a world of ever-evolving change and uncertainty. The challenges that leaders face today have never been seen before. That's why effective leadership matters now more than ever. As a leader, you're called to serve. You are called to set an example for others. You are called to motivate and inspire your people. When you're a leader, people watch what you say and do. Your actions speak louder than your words. There are rewards and consequences for what you do. Your actions can build people up or tear them down. The right action, taken at the right point in time, can thrust an organization forward. On the other hand, one wrong decision can have a lasting negative effect on your people.

Vision is about developing a clear sense of mission and purpose that provides direction to others. Leaders who clearly translate and communicate vision, goals, and priorities in a simple and succinct manner get buy-in and commitment from their people. They create alignment by communicating what's most important. When they model and reinforce the vision, employees understand how their responsibilities tie into the bigger picture. Visionary leaders are strong strategic thinkers. They are bright and analytical. They can quickly assimilate and synthesize complex processes and information. They see future trends and patterns that will impact their business. When leaders set the vision, they help people understand why the company's desired outcomes are so important.

Passion is about demonstrating a positive and optimistic sense of energy and enthusiasm for people to follow. Passionate leaders operate with a never-ending desire to be the best in their area of expertise. They are fully engaged in their work. They talk beyond today and anticipate new possibilities for their people, teams, and organizations. They rally people behind a core mission and purpose. Passionate leaders are also action-oriented and decisive. They take a hands-on approach to their work. They keep people motivated and focused on the right priorities. They manage resistance and fear of change at all levels with openness, clarity, and objectivity. They are optimistic and hopeful. This encourages people to do the same. Passionate leaders are highly self-motivated. They actively encourage and reinforce the right mindset to drive success.

Commitment is about persevering with confidence and composure under difficult and high-stress situations. Committed leaders have the fortitude to stay the course and make tough decisions for the benefits of the enterprise. They create viable feedback loops with key stakeholders to anticipate needs and track performance. They focus the necessary resources on priorities that will improve current processes and procedures. Committed leaders are comfortable with ambiguity. They foster clarity of purpose and prioritization during times of change and uncertainty. They persist in overcoming obstacles from all sources—from the organization, from their team, from customers, and from senior leadership.

Vigilant leaders demonstrate personal accountability and ownership for decisions, results, and consequences. They establish role clarity and accountabilities regarding deliverables, time lines, and key milestones. They use structure, process, and clear expectations to keep people focused on the right priorities. They prioritize effectively so that the best use of talent, time, and resources can be allocated to the right issues. They instill a sense of urgency. They tackle problems head on and take decisive action to drive results. Vigilance is about challenging yourself and others to improve processes for greater long-term impact. When leaders are vigilant, they consistently exceed expectations and goals. They deliver results that raise the bar on performance. They do not allow competing demands to take away from their goals.

Consistency is about leading with character, courage, and integrity at all times. Consistent leaders remain calm under pressure and deliver on their commitments. They communicate good and bad news in a straightforward and honest way. They demonstrate the courage of their convictions. They know when to listen and when to press a point. They understand and embrace the burdens as well as the benefits of leadership. Consistent leaders pragmatically deal with situations in an emotionally mature and even-handed manner. They are motivated by more than personal gain and advancement. They promote the greater good of the organization. They respect and value core attributes of the company's culture while proactively seeking to enhance it. They inspire trust through both words and actions.

Endurance is about having stamina, resilience, and tenacity to achieve one's goals. Leaders who possess endurance remain persistent under adversity and setbacks. They effectively delegate responsibilities to team members in order to maximize efforts toward goal attainment. They know how to play at the right level. They empower others to make and own decisions within their areas of responsibility. When leaders have endurance, they thrive under pressure. They have effective strategies and resources for managing pressure and stress. They can readily shift attention between strategic and tactical issues. They get to the root causes of problems and find solutions to continually generate productive results. They create cultures where people are decisive about what needs to be done rather than waiting to be told what to do.

Compassionate leaders have an impact on people through communication, social awareness, and relational intelligence. They build trust by using their emotional intelligence to understand the emotions and well-being of others. They empathize with the experiences of others and do not overly rely on their personal experience. Compassionate leaders have the ability to connect with others and build long-term sustainable relationships. They take time to establish rapport with new colleagues. They understand people and value individual differences. They value diversity. They use their influence for good. They possess a deep understanding and the ability to anticipate the needs of others through listening and observation. Compassionate leaders also know what people are good at and put them in situations where they will succeed. They understand their employees' strengths and weaknesses and actively coach and mentor people to develop their capabilities.

Inspirational leaders motivate, encourage, and influence others to drive results. They give people something to believe in and establish a rallying cry for the organization. They inspire followership. They attract, retain, and engage a diverse and talented workforce. They empower employees by providing them with the freedom and autonomy to make appropriate decisions. They earn people's trust by delivering on promises and reducing barriers and restrictions to information exchange. They challenge and invite challenge from others. They encourage diversity of thinking to get to superior outcomes. Inspirational leaders possess sufficient humility to appropriately compromise with others to achieve results. They use the right incentives and rewards to motivate desired behaviors from their people. They collaborate and encourage collaboration across all levels of their organization.

Innovation is about applying continuous improvements to processes and procedures over time. Innovative leaders refine goals and objectives along the way. They drive the creativity needed to effectively manage the rapid pace of change. They have the ability to see problems from multiple angles and can effectively evaluate options. They draw high-quality conclusions. When leaders are innovative, they take a nimble approach to anticipating and responding to changes in their operating landscape. They course correct with new data and changing market conditions. They spot patterns and trends that have a large impact on the organization. They reward and celebrate the creativity of others. They take charge in seeking and leveraging new opportunities. They take calculated risks to lead rather than follow the industry. Innovative leaders love the stimulation of intellectual challenges and learning new subject matter to improve performance.

Wisdom is about understanding how today's decisions will impact tomorrow. Wise leaders can translate an understanding of industry, customers, and competitors to broad strategic choices for the organization. They think about the business from a holistic perspective. They anticipate downstream impact of decisions on customers, employees, and the financials. Wise leaders lead with a global mind-set. They think outside their personal cultural mind-set. They are willing to take calculated risks, make mistakes, and learn from them. They demonstrate strong business acumen. They set a tone of learning for others from both successes and failures. They draw appropriate parallels and linkages from past experience. They constantly look for ways to develop and grow.

Your Leadership Self-Assessment

We've covered the ten key leadership competencies in great detail in this book. Each one plays a critical role in your leadership. So where do you stand on each area? Are you a visionary leader? Do you lead with passion and commitment? Are you consistent, and do you lead with integrity? Do you have the stamina and resilience to push through obstacles to achieve your goals? Are you compassionate and inspirational? Do you value innovation? Do you consider yourself to be a wise leader? As an organizational psychologist, I love to develop assessment tools that help my clients get a deep understanding of their talents and capabilities. It gives them a baseline of identifying their strengths and areas of opportunity. This helps leaders to create their personal development plans. It gives them the opportunity to work on their leadership. It helps them to grow.

Now it's your turn. Below is the *What Every Leader Needs* self-assessment. There are five questions for each competency area. I strongly encourage you to answer the questions openly and honestly. This is about your leadership. No one is going to see your scores. This is for your personal growth and development. The scoring key is as follows:

1 = Never
2 = Rarely
3 = Sometimes
4 = Often
5 = Always

Enter your scores for each question. After you have completed each section, add up your scores for that competency. Remember, if you're fully honest and truthful with yourself, you will get the most out of this exercise.

Vision

I am the type of leader who…

1. Creates a clear and concise vision that connects our customers, our employees, and financial outcomes. _____
2. Clearly translates and communicates vision, goals, and priorities in a simple and succinct manner. _____
3. Provides sound business judgment and strategic thinking to colleagues across all levels of the organization. _____
4. Thinks about and defines a positive future state of the business. _____
5. Can adjust a message to meet the knowledge and skill level of the audience. _____

Total Score _____

Passion

I am the type of leader who...

1. Brings a passionate commitment and energy to challenges. _____

2. Conveys a sense of urgency and enthusiasm throughout the company to support growth. ____

3. Inspires followership with personal energy and conviction. _____

4. Excites people with ideas and new ways of thinking. _____

5. Motivates people to do things they would otherwise never try to do. _____

Total Score _____

Commitment

I am the type of leader who...

1. Persists in overcoming obstacles and challenges from all potential sources. _____

2. Is persistent in driving change initiatives to upgrade systems, processes, and talent. _____

3. Properly sequences and socializes ideas to minimize resistance. _____

4. Focuses on the critical few priorities for the business to drive long-term success. _____

5. Makes adjustments to vision and strategy as needed while remaining focused on key outcomes. _____

Total Score _____

Vigilance

I am the type of leader who...

1. Holds people accountable for results and how they are accomplished. _____
2. Directly tackles internal and external obstacles to execution. _____
3. Drives a sense of urgency and direction to exceed expectations. _____
4. Takes personal ownership for taking vision and strategy to execution. _____
5. Ensures accountability through regular follow-up and providing timely, direct, and actionable feedback. _____

Total Score _____

Consistency

I am the type of leader who...

1. Creates conditions of complete openness and transparency. _____
2. Establishes credibility and impact through presence and demeanor. _____
3. Is transparent and open with information appropriately with different groups. _____
4. Has an openness to feedback and a willingness to change when necessary. _____
5. Demonstrates unquestionable ethics and integrity. _____

Total Score _____

Endurance

I am the type of leader who...

1. Empowers people to make and own decisions within their areas of responsibility. _____
2. Leads with resilience, fortitude, and stamina. _____
3. Translates setbacks into opportunities. _____
4. Displays tenacity and takes proactive measures to make improvements. _____
5. Establishes and maintains appropriate governance toward the attainment of goals. _____

Total Score _____

Compassion

I am the type of leader who...

1. Leads with empathy and relational intelligence. _____
2. Creates in others the capacity for continuous improvement. _____
3. Is candid, present, and grounded, with a sincere respect for the experience of others. _____
4. Creates a climate of transparency by setting a positive example for others. _____
5. Actively develops people through coaching, actionable constructive feedback, and growth assignments. _____

Total Score _____

Inspiration

I am the type of leader who…

1. Inspires trust through both words and actions. _____
2. Moves people emotionally when talking with them. _____
3. Influences without always having to be the leader of an effort. _____
4. Has the ability to engage, inspire, and motivate people to achieve goals. _____
5. Collaborates and encourages collaboration across the team and organization. _____

Total Score _____

Innovation

I am the type of leader who…

1. Continuously looks for ways to improve processes and procedures to drive greater efficiencies. _____
2. Operates with a deep level of curiosity and inquisitiveness. _____
3. Fosters an environment that promotes continuous learning and growth. _____
4. Challenges established ways of thinking in a constructive fashion. _____
5. Is open to new ideas and ways of doing things that challenge existing processes. _____

Total Score _____

Wisdom

I am the type of leader who...

1. Leads with a global perspective and thinks outside of my cultural background. _____
2. Sees through complexity and considers alternatives to finding the best possible path forward for the organization. _____
3. Can translate an understanding of industry, customers, and competitors to broad strategic choices for the business. _____
4. Balances big, conceptual thinking with pragmatism and focus. _____
5. Spots patterns and anticipates future trends that may impact the organization. _____

Total Score _____

Interpreting Your Scores

Now that you have taken the assessment, let's see how you did. Total scores between 5 and 10 is a *Leadership Gap*. This is an area that you need to spend a lot of time on if you want to grow and improve. Total scores between 11 and 15 is a *Needs Improvement* area. You have some skills here but can do some work to further your development in that competency area. Total scores between a 16 and 20 is a *Proficient Skill*. You're strong in this area and should leverage the competency in your leadership. There might be small tweaks that you can make to further improve. Total scores between a 21 and 25 is a *Towering Strength*. These are your top leadership competencies. These are the behaviors that you should instill and encourage in others. You're at the level where you can offer guidance and support to others to further their understanding and growth.

Your Leadership Journey

Taking the assessment is the first step in your leadership development journey. Now that you know where you stand in each of the competencies, it's time to put together your personal development game plan. When I work with clients, we will first go through the assessment phase. This is where the leader will get a thorough understanding of their strengths and development opportunities. That is what you just did by completing the *What Every Leader Needs* self-assessment. The second, and more critical step, is putting together your personal development plan. As an example and illustration, we will use two of the ten competency areas as developmental opportunities. Let's say you scored the lowest on vigilance and wisdom. These two leadership skills would be your areas for growth.

We will start with vigilance. Go back to the five questions for vigilance. What questions did you score the lowest on? Perhaps you scored lowest on "Ensures accountability through regular follow-up and providing timely, direct, and actionable feedback" and "Drives a sense of urgency and direction to exceed expectations." If this was the case, your development opportunity could be holding people accountable for results. If I was your coach, we would set a goal around finding ways to hold people accountable. That would be the primary objective. Next, I would have you draw two lines dividing a piece of paper into four quadrants. In the upper left-hand corner of the page, we would title that section *Behaviors and Actions*. In this section, I would have you list key behaviors that you would start to put in place to accomplish the goal. For example, you could start having biweekly one-on-one meetings with each of your direct reports to track progress against their projects and key performance objectives. You could also start having monthly team meetings to evaluate how the group is progressing toward collective objectives for the business. You could also build out an excel spreadsheet to track progress of all your team members goals. The behaviors have to be specific and actionable. They cannot be vague or too general.

In the upper-right quadrant of the document, you would title that section *Impact*. Here you will focus on the impact your goal will

have on the business. For example, if you are able to more consistently hold your team members accountable, your team will be able
to accomplish their goals faster. You will deliver on the expectations
that your boss has set for you and your team. You will be able to
identify stretch assignments and projects to elevate the talent and
capabilities of your people.

In the bottom left-hand quadrant, you would title that section
Obstacles. Here you identify what challenges could get in the way
of you achieving your primary objective. You could list things like
getting distracted by too many demands of the business. Perhaps you
could get wrapped up in your own priorities that you miss having the
regular one-on-ones with your people. You might have to reduce the
number of resources that are available to your team to accomplish
their goals. You have to be specific in this section. So many leaders
miss this step and then get frustrated later on when they are not able
to achieve their development objective. By identifying the obstacles
that can get in your way, you can be more proactive to take action to
prevent them from occurring.

In the bottom-right-hand quadrant, you will title this section
Progress/Success Markers. Here is where you will list the key milestones
that will help you determine if the behaviors and actions you put
in place are actually working. In this section, you can write about
weekly, monthly, or quarterly observable results. Perhaps, you want
to keep track of sales and performance goals. Did your team get their
sales target for the quarter? Maybe you want to determine if your
team was able to develop a new product. Did you meet the project deadline for developing it? Make sure the progress and success
factors are observable. You want to be able to come back to your
development plan later on and ensure that the behaviors you put in
place helped you get to your desired outcomes. This is a great way to
reinforce that your efforts are actually having an impact.

For wisdom, you would follow the same process. First, go back
to the questions in that section of the assessment. Your lowest scores
were "Leads with a global perspective and thinks outside my cultural background" and "Can translate an understanding of industry,
customers, and competitors to broad strategic choices for the busi-

ness." After reviewing these results, you might want to set a primary objective of improving your strategic capabilities. For the *Behaviors and Actions* section, you could focus on identifying a few mentors in other lines of business to broaden your understanding of enterprise priorities. If you live in the US, you could get involved in a project with a cross-functional team outside of the country. Perhaps your organization has an international business and working with colleagues in that area would strengthen your strategic capabilities.

For *Impact*, you could list things like understanding how to better serve the customers in your region. Maybe being more strategic will enable you to drive greater profitable growth. You could develop a greater understanding of how your company stays on the cutting edge and competes with other companies in your industry. For *Obstacles*, you could list things like getting pulled into tactical responsibilities of your role. You might not be able to identify the right mentors who will help you grow. You could get reassigned to a new project that would take up all your time. Lastly, for *Progress/ Success Markers*, you could list things like getting a promotion in a quicker time frame. You could be asked to join larger strategic initiative for the organization. Maybe you will get an opportunity to take on new role in a different business unit.

Make sure your primary objectives are things that you want to work on. It is hard to stick to a development plan if you are not committed to your goals. Engage your manager in the process so that they can serve as a thought partner in helping you reach your desired outcomes. Maybe you want to work with an executive coach. Having an external resource that is outside your organization might help you navigate some of the challenges that could surface along the way. I'm a firm believer that every leader should have a coach. Cultivating the talent and skills needed to have long-term impact requires focus, discipline, and effort. A coach will partner with you to help guide you along the journey.

If you're going to work with an executive coach, you want someone who meshes well with your style and personality. You want a coach who is results-oriented. They should always link your personal development objectives to strategic priorities of your role and organization. You want a coach that is honest, direct, and candid. A good coach should be supportive but also challenge you in your thinking. Trust with your coach is also critical. If you don't feel that you can establish a trusting partnership with your coach, you will not be receptive to their feedback.

Coaching engagements can last anywhere from six months to a year. The length of a coaching engagement usually depends on your goals, and the progress that you are making against your desired outcomes. A skilled executive coach should help strengthen your self-awareness. They should work with you to create an actionable personal development plan. They should be able to help you achieve real results and long-term shifts in performance. If you're interested in learning more and working with an executive coach, you can visit our website, www.bandelliandassociates.com, for further information. We have a number of resources that outlines our coaching process and how to find the right coach for you.

Building a Reputation of Leadership Excellence

You have to earn your leadership every day. Reputation is built on repetition and relationship. As a leader, you have to do the same consistent things day in and day out to garner the respect, buy-in, and commitment from your people. That's how you build a strong leadership reputation. That's how you leave a lasting positive impact on others. It's repetition in what you do in each and every one of your working relationships. When it comes to reputation, you have to stick to your values and beliefs. Don't stray from who you are at your core. Make sure the same you shows up on both good and bad days.

Great leaders develop reputations over time. Their influence is forged in the big important moments. For example, when a crisis hits, they are decisive and take action. When challenges are presented to the organization, they respond with courage and dignity. When obstacles arise, they are fearless and inspire commitment from their people. It's also about the details and the little things. It's about taking time to sit down one-on-one and check in with your team members. It's the thoughtful e-mail or compliment when someone achieves a goal. It's making yourself available to your people when they need guidance and support. Excellence is a word that we hear a lot about today. Some tell us to strive for excellence in all that we do. Others encourage us to focus on excellence and not perfection. I believe excellence is achieved in how you show up for your people. When leaders put others first, they build cultures of excellence. As leaders, we are called to a higher standard. What we do emanates down through our organizations. The impact we have on people is what really matters most.

As I reflect on my career to date, there have been a number of leaders who have left a positive impact on my life. Each individual leader whom I've coached has taught me a valuable lesson in leadership. One of the most impactful leaders whom I have worked with is David, a CEO of a pharmaceuticals company in North America. David and I started our relationship back when he was a vice president of sales for a medical devices organization. David was a rare breed. He was the son of first-generation immigrants from Europe. He grew up in a poor environment. His parents had to work extremely hard to earn a living. His father owned a small tailoring business in New York City. The business struggled for many years; but he learned about discipline, dedication to one's craft, and perseverance. David was fascinated by people. He would go to work with his father on a regular basis and study their customers. He was a curious child and always asked questions to learn about people's backgrounds and experiences.

During his educational years, he gravitated toward business. He was a hard worker and paid his way through college. He worked three jobs while balancing his academic responsibilities. David started his career as a sales rep for a small biotech pharmaceutical company. It was during this time that he cultivated and sharpened his people skills. David was charismatic. He found ways to connect with people from all walks of life. This wasn't an act. He genuinely valued and cared for others. His focus on building relationships with customers helped establish his early success. Year after year, he was in the top ten percent of the company's sales performance.

People trusted David. This afforded him more opportunities of influence. He quickly became a regional manager and started overseeing the activities of others. As a leader, he always put people first. He knew that the business results meant nothing if he didn't have employees that felt valued and appreciated. So he took the time to invest in the development of his people. He was always looking for ways help them learn. He took pride in getting his direct reports promoted and advancing their careers. This became part of his reputation. He was known for accelerating the growth of his employees and helping them to exceed performance expectations.

Our work began when he was brought into the medical devices company as a vice president. As part of his onboarding and integration to the organization, I served as his executive coach. We quickly formed a strong bond and partnership. He viewed me as a trusted advisor because I was always honest and direct with him. I was authentic in our work together and never pulled any punches. David valued our candid conversations and was always eager to improve. As our partnership has spanned over fifteen years, I've seen David grow in many ways. He's also helped make me a better consultant and leader in my firm.

I have learned three valuable lessons from working with David. First, servant leadership is the best way to get the most out of your people. When people know you are in their corner and will always go to bat for them, they want to do their best for you. David always put his people first. This garnered loyalty and commitment from his teams. His people knew that his top priority was their success and well-being. Second, relational intelligence is more important than one's technical talents and capabilities. David was a smart individual. He was strategic, had good business acumen, and had a deep understanding of the business. However, it was his ability to build relationships with people from all walks of life that drove his success. He was warm and genuine when meeting new people. He was compassionate and found ways to empathize with others. I saw this firsthand with many of his people and their customers.

Lastly, David made learning his lifelong pursuit. He was always looking for new ways to grow. He was humble and admitted when he didn't know certain things. He leveraged the guidance and insights of others. Throughout his career, he consistently looked for ways to sharpen his game. Whether it was learning a new product and technology or figuring out how to connect in different ways with his customers, he looked for ways to innovate and improve. He always encouraged and rewarded his people for doing the same. Over the course of our relationship, I have seen many of his people come up with new ideas and grow their business. This has happened because of his willingness to encourage diversity of thinking in his people. Your reputation as a leader is built over time. When you put people first, focus more on relationships rather than results, and strive to learn and grow, you leave a lasting impression on others.

Your Leadership Legacy

What is happening in you is always more important than what's happening to you. As a leader, the challenges you face today develops the strength you need for tomorrow. Yes, talent will land you a good job. High performance will surely get you promoted. But it is your character that makes you a great leader. People will always follow a leader with a heart, faster than they will follow one with a title or position of power.

Leadership is about influence. Influence is the ability to impact people's decisions and actions. If you have influence, you help move your employees forward. You build a legacy when you have a positive impact on the lives of others. Your steady leadership helps them form opinions, make decisions, and take actions that can change the world around them. When you're impactful, you add value to people's lives. That's something that can last long after you're gone.

So what is the mark you want to leave on the world? The mark you want to leave on your people and your organization? What do you want to have been known for? What do you want others to say about you? As leaders, these are the critical questions we have to ask ourselves. When you start to figure these things out, you're well on your way to having a positive impact on others. Every leader needs to grow. By learning and putting our ten competencies into practice, you will improve as a leader. Regardless of your industry or profession, these leadership skills will help you have the influence you want to have with your people.

The great Athenian philosopher Plato once said, "The first and best victory is to conquer self." In leadership, you have to fully commit to a lifelong journey of growth and development. You need good self-awareness. You have to understand your strengths and opportunity areas. You need to surround yourself with people you trust—those who will be honest and candid with you, those who will hold you accountable to the standards you set for the organization. The future belongs to the leaders who are constantly looking for ways to improve. When leaders grow, everyone around them gets better. Leaders who are quick to apply what they learn have the greatest long-term success. They get the best out of their people, teams, and organizations.

ABOUT THE AUTHOR

D r. Adam C. Bandelli is Managing Director of Bandelli & Associates. Adam has twenty years of management and consulting experience in the firm's service offerings, including board consultation, senior executive selection, leadership development, pre-investment due diligence, organizational culture and transformational change. As an expert on executive leadership and relational intelligence, Adam works with CEOs and senior executives to strengthen their abilities to inspire and influence their people, teams, and organizations. Adam has worked with leaders around the world in organizations ranging from small start-up firms through global Fortune 100 companies. He has consulted to a diverse set of industry sectors including, private equity, financial services, consumer products, manufacturing, medical devices, retail, energy, pharmaceuticals, sports and entertainment, nonprofit, and telecommunications.

Prior to founding Bandelli & Associates, Adam was a Partner at Korn Ferry, where he led the Private Equity assessment practice for North America. Earlier in his career, he was a Partner at RHR International, where he served as one of the firm's leaders on CEO Succession and Leadership Development. Adam received his Ph.D. and master's degrees from the University of South Florida in Industrial-Organizational Psychology, and a bachelor's degree concentrating in Psychology and Business Management from Fairleigh Dickinson University. Acknowledged as a world-renowned thought leader on transformational leadership and organizational effectiveness, he is a frequent speaker at Fortune 500 companies, leadership retreats, and business and professional meetings.

Adam lives in New Jersey with his wife Kat and their son Stephen. As a former athlete, Adam spends his recreational time long distance running and weight training. He has competed in several marathons including the TCS New York City Marathon. He is an avid golfer and is usually spending his weekends on the golf course. His family are active members in their church, ChurchAlive, and volunteer in their local community.

For more information on Adam, his firm, and their leadership advisory consulting service offerings visit www.bandelliandassociates.com. **Leadership Matters. Without It, People Fail.**

CPSIA information can be obtained
at www.ICGtesting.com
Printed in the USA
LVHW030348100421
684048LV00006B/9/J

9 781636 301372